The Complete Book of

SOLITAIRE
AND
PATIENCE

D0916606

The Complete Book of
SOLITAIRE
AND
PATIENCE

Albert Morehead and Geoffrey Mott-Smith

foulsham
LONDON • NEW YORK • TORONTO • SYDNEY

foulsham

The Publishing House, Bennetts Close,
Cippenham, Slough, Berkshire, SL1 5AP, England

ISBN 0-572-02654-4

Printed in Great Britain by St. Edmundsbury Press, Bury St. Edmunds, Suffolk.

Contents

About Solitaire Games – and about this Book

It is natural to think that solitaire games preceded card games for two or more players. We can easily imagine how solitaire grew out of the rites of dealing and selecting the cards for fortune telling, while divination is the first known use of the tarot cards. But this is really just guesswork, as there are very few historical records concerning solitaire.

Scholars disagree about the ultimate origin of playing cards, but it is generally thought that they were introduced during the 14th century to northern Europe, probably from Italy. We do know the main rules of a game played at that time, *tarocchini* or *tarok*, which is still played in central Europe. But not until the 19th century did anyone bother to record the rules of a solitaire game for posterity.

The playing of patience is referred to in Tolstoy's *War and Peace*, in a scene supposed to have taken place in 1808. As Tolstoy was very careful about his historical details, this reference is unlikely to be inaccurate, particularly as Tolstoy himself was a passionate devotee of solitaire.

However, there are probably much earlier references to solitaire in French literature, since the earliest English books on patience seem to have drawn on French sources. Indeed, the very names of the games in these books are almost all French – La Belle Lucie, Les Quatre Coins, L'Horloge, La Nivernaise, La Loi Salique, Le Carré Napoléon, etc.

As well, there is a newsletter dated 1816, which reported that Napoleon Bonaparte, in exile at St Helena, kept himself busy 'playing patience'. This is the earliest reference to patience as a game, unearthed by the *Oxford English Dictionary*, though Patience seems to have been such a well-known game that it needed no further explanation.

Whether Napoleon invented any of the games bearing his name, or even whether or not he played them, no-one really knows. Perhaps they were older games, renamed for Napoleon by his admirers. During his brilliant military campaigns in Italy and Austria, thousands of commercial products changed to the brand 'Napoleon'. Alternatively, the Napoleon solitaires may have been invented during this extraordinarily fertile and rich period of experimentation and innovation in playing cards. Interestingly, it was about this time that the ace (symbolising the lowest social class) began to be placed regularly above the king (the nobility), and old designs gave way to new symbols of the French Revolution. At some gambling casinos, the faces of the cards changed daily, while the 'house rule' for ranking the cards changed three times a week.

Many new games, and new variants of old games, were invented during this period. The solitaire family of card games probably also flourished during this time, but again there is a sad lack of historical records.

There is no reference to solitaire, much less the description of a particular patience, in any of the books upon which the modern day relies for its early history of card games, such as Charles Cotton's *The Compleat Gamester* (1674), Abbé Bellecour's *Academie des Jeux* (1768) and *Bohn's Handbook of Games* (1850).

The first English compendium of solitaire games is believed to be Lady Adelaide Cadogan's *Illustrated Games of Patience*, published in about 1870 – a pioneer work that ran through many editions. At about the same time Mrs E.D. Cheney wrote *Patience* and Annie B. Henshaw wrote *Amusements for Invalids* (Boston 1870). Soon, the publishers of handbooks on chess, whist, croquet, badminton, etc., were busy adding solitaire to their book lists. In 1883, Dick & Fitzgerald of New York issued their first series of *Dick's Games of Patience,* followed by a second series in 1898. These well-printed, illustrated volumes greatly added to the list of recorded solitaires.

By the end of the 19th century, there were many books on solitaire. Among those who made important contributions were 'Cavendish' (H.E. Jones), 'Professor Hoffmann' (Angelo Lewis), Basil Dalton and Ernest Bergholt.

Another literary reference published about this time can be found in Somerset Maugham's *The Gentleman in the Parlour:* 'I reproached myself as I set out the cards. Considering the shortness of life and the infinite number of important things there are to do during its course, it can only be the proof of a flippant disposition that one should waste one's time in such a pursuit … But I knew seventeen varieties of patience. I tried the Spider and never by any chance got it out …'

It might be wondered whether this self-reproach was sincere. After all, it is not necessarily 'proof of a flippant disposition' to take recreation. There is a well-known statesman – who, at moments of crisis, tended to relax with solitaire. Oddly enough, he too was a devotee of Spider. At the time he was President of the USA. He was Franklin Delano Roosevelt.

The catharsis of patience has been recognised by many novelists. Tolstoy himself had an addiction to patience bordering on superstition. At times of uncertainty, he would play a card game to decide what to do, though it is said if he did not like the answer, he would reshuffle and deal again. Another Russian author, Dostoevsky, in *The Brothers Karamazov,* portrays the character, Grushenka, resorting to solitaire to get through an almost unbearable period of suspense. The game played by Grushenka was called Fools.

Another game, which became almost a common noun at one time, is Canfield. The game is named after Mr Canfield, who owned a fashionable gambling salon in Saratoga in the last decade of the 19th century. He proposed that players buy a deck of cards for $50 and play a game of the solitaire Canfield. He pledged to pay a player $5 for every card in their foundation piles at the end of play. Since the player could expect on average between five and six cards, this meant Mr Canfield stood to win about $25 per game. Despite this inordinate house percentage, thousands of players accepted Mr Canfield's proposition, and the cult of Canfield spread all over the country. Mr Canfield is believed to have accumulated a small fortune in this way, though he later said his solitaire room was less lucrative than the roulette wheel. While only two housemen were needed to operate roulette and could therefore handle lots of customers at any one time, a houseman had to be hired for every solitaire punter to watch the player for fraud.

The game played at Canfield's casino is the game described in this book as 'Canfield' (see page 25). However, Canfield has also been a name widely misapplied to another game, Klondike, which eventually overtook Canfield in popularity.

How to choose a Solitaire Game

Solitaires differ widely in the opportunities they provide for the exercise of skill. Some, like Block Eleven, are purely mechanical. Others, like Sly Fox, can probably be won against any fall of the cards, using sufficient patience and foresight. Many, like Calculation, call for utmost skill which is often cancelled out by bad luck.

It is no slur upon a solitaire to say that it is purely mechanical or gives little scope for skill. Indeed, the games of this type are the most restful. But IF you wish to pit your wits against the luck of the deal, IF you wish to bedevil your brain with tortuous calculation, here is a list for your guidance.

The following lists of 'Solitaires of Skill' represent, of course, the personal opinion of the authors. But special attention has been given to certain objective criteria. To give reasonable scope for skill, a game must give choices of play in sufficient number and frequency. Furthermore, these choices must obviously have an effect on the outcome. No game that has a slight chance of being won – say worse than one chance in ten – can be a game of skill, because the choices will not have sufficient effect on the outcome.

The games are listed alphabetically; we have not tried to rank them against each other.

SOLITAIRES GIVING MAXIMUM OPPORTUNITY FOR SKILL

One pack (deck)

Baker's Dozen	58
Beleaguered Castle	40-1
Bristol	95-6
Calculation	78-9
Eight Off	96-7
Fission	97-8
Flower Garden	46-7
Good Measure	58
La Belle Lucie	49-50
Little Spider	59-60
Poker Solitaire	101
Shamrocks	51
Strategy	99-100
Trefoil	50
Yukon	48

Two packs (decks)

Big Ben	169-70
British Square	161-2
Constitution	112-13
Cornerstones	130-1
Crazy Quilt	146-8
Crescent	162-3
Frog	110-11
Gavotte	145
House on the Hill	134
House in the Wood	134
Intelligence	133
Maria	115
Sly Fox	108-9
Spider	107-8
Terrace	138-40
Tournament	123-4
Virginia Reel	125-70

Other

SOLITAIRES GIVING MODERATE OPPORTUNITY FOR SKILL

One pack (deck)

Two packs (decks)

Four packs (decks)

General Procedure of Solitaire

(With explanation of terms)

Cards All solitaires are based on the standard pack of 52 cards. Most solitaires use either one pack, or two packs shuffled together. A few use more than two packs; a few others use one pack reduced to 40, 32 or 20 cards, or the Pinochle pack, which is actually two packs stripped to the nines.

This book also includes solitaire games using the joker, a fifty-third card added to the standard pack.

For nearly all solitaires, it is important that the pack is thoroughly shuffled before dealing begins.

Suits and sequence The standard pack comprises 13 cards of four suits: spades (♠), hearts (♥), diamonds (♦) and clubs (♣).

The cards in each suit are: A, 2, 3, 4, 5, 6, 7, 8, 9, 10, J, Q, K. This order is the basic rank from low (ace) to high (king). In many cases the ranking is continuous, that is, the ace is in sequence above the king as well as below the two. In a few cases the sequence has top and bottom limits other than king and ace. All such variations from the basic sequence are noted in the text of this book.

When the cards are considered as numerical quantities, the king is 13, the queen 12, the jack 11 and the ace 1.

Layout Many solitaires begin with the dealing of a fixed number of cards upon the table, in some conventional pattern. Cards dealt in this way are called the *layout*.

Where any cards of the layout are dealt face down, the fact is noted in this book. In the absence of such a note, deal all cards face up.

Common layout patterns are 'rows' and 'columns' which may or may not be 'overlapped'; there are also 'piles' and 'fans'. For ease of reference, certain groups of cards in the layout may be designated as 'foundations', 'tableau', 'reserve' or by descriptive terms such as 'wing'. Particular terms are explained when they occur; the general terms are defined and illustrated on the following pages.

Row A line of cards parallel to the edge of the table at which the player is seated.

A row is dealt from left to right. If if is *overlapped*, each card is laid upon that previously dealt, so as to cover most of its face but leaving the index in the upper left corner visible. The 'top card' or 'right end' of an overlapped row is the card that would be uppermost if the row were pushed together into a pile.

Column A line of cards perpendicular to the edge of the table at which the player is seated.

A column is dealt from the point farthest from the player, towards himself. The far point is the *top*, being nearest the top of the page in a diagram; the card nearest the player is at the bottom of the diagram and is referred to as the 'bottom card'.

If the cards in a column are *overlapped*, each card is laid upon that previously dealt so as to cover most of its face but leaving the index in the upper left corner visible. To avoid ambiguity as to which is then the 'bottom' card, a column of overlapping cards is referred to, in this book, as a *spread pile* or a *pile spread downwards;* and the top card of the pile is that card which is not covered in whole or in part by any other.

Pile A batch of cards dealt upon each other and squared up in a compact heap.

A series of piles is often dealt by laying out a row or column, then another row or column on top of the first, and so on.

The object in making a pile, instead of overlapping the cards, may be either (a) to save room, or (b) to prevent more than one card at a time being visible. In case (b), the pile should usually be dealt face down, then squared and turned face up. In the absence of a specific rule to the contrary, any pile of face-up cards may be spread for inspection of lower cards.

ELEMENTS OF THE LAYOUT

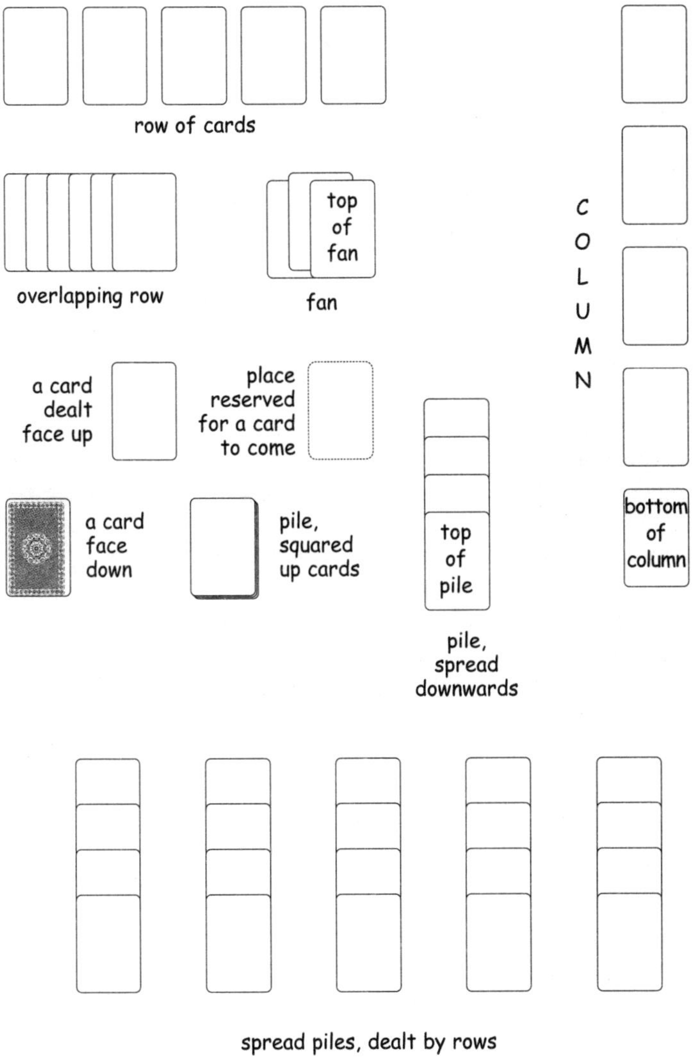

row of cards

overlapping row

top of fan

fan

C
O
L
U
M
N

a card dealt face up

place reserved for a card to come

a card face down

pile, squared up cards

top of pile

pile, spread downwards

bottom of column

spread piles, dealt by rows

The top card of a pile is that card which is not covered by any other.

Fan An overlapped row, usually made by counting the cards off the pack face down, then spreading them face up with a sweep of the hand.

Foundation The first cards of certain piles, where the object of play is to build the entire pack upon these piles.

Most solitaires – though not all – use foundations. When the foundations are part of the layout, you are directed to 'Remove (certain cards) from the pack and put them in a (row or column)'. When the foundations are not part of the layout, you are directed to 'Move (certain cards), as they become available, to a (row or column)'.

The foundations are usually all the cards of a specified rank (often aces). Sometimes the rank is fixed by chance in the deal; in a few cases, the foundations are cards of different ranks.

Whenever foundations are used, assume the following rules apply unless certain exceptions are specifically noted:

(1) A card once built on a foundation may not be moved elsewhere.

(2) A foundation card may not be built upon until it is in the foundation row; usually it must be moved to the foundation row as soon as it becomes available (unless it was prefixed there).

(3) Building in other parts of the layout stops at the rank next to the foundation cards. For example, if aces are foundations, and there is building downwards in the tableau, nothing may be built on a two and a king may not be built on any other card.

(4) When the foundation is other than ace or king, these two cards are in sequence. For example, if sevens are foundations, the sequence of rank is: 7 (low), 8, 9, 10, J, Q, K, A, 2, 3, 4, 5, 6 (high).

Winning a game At this point, we might as well explain what is meant by 'winning' a solitaire game.

Whenever foundations are used the object of play is to build the entire pack upon them and the game is won if this object is achieved. When there are no foundations, the objective that constitutes winning is stated specifically.

Whether 'partial winning' exists is a subjective matter. If you play the game of Canfield for recreation, you may consider that you have lost if you do not 'get out' all 52 cards; but had you played for stakes against Mr Canfield himself you would have been happy – and a winner – to get out 11 or more cards. In the case of some of the solitaires with long odds for winning, this book gives scoring methods that allow for degrees of victory.

Reserve, Tableau These terms designate parts of the layout other than foundations. Rigid definition would impair their usefulness. But on a *reserve* no building is ever allowed; on a *tableau* building is usually allowed, though not invariably.

Spaces Wherever a reserve or tableau is made up of separate cards, piles or overlapped rows, the entire removal of any such unit (including cards built upon it) leaves a *space*. The rules of each game state whether and how a space may be filled. In many solitaires, the chief opportunity for skill is in the use of spaces.

Stock This is the remainder of the pack, after the layout is dealt. The stock must always be kept in a pile, face down.

The stock is brought into play in either of two ways: (a) cards are turned up from it one at a time, each becoming available for building as it is turned up; (b) cards are dealt into spaces, or dealt upon the original layout in added batches.

Wastepile When cards from the stock may be added to the layout only under certain restrictions as to building, the unplayable cards are laid face up in one or more *wastepiles*. Cards placed in a wastepile may be brought back into play later; usually, the top card of a wastepile is available for play.

Building Placing one card upon another in the foundations or tableau, under certain restrictions.

Any of the following rules may apply as to suit:

(1) *Regardless of suit.* Building is governed by rank alone; any seven may be built on any eight.

(2) *In suit.* For example, a space only on another space; with due attention, of course, to any rules concerning the rank of the cards.

(3) *In colour.* A black card only on another black card, a red card only on another red card. For example, a spade can be placed on either a spade or a club.

(4) *In alternate colours.* A black card only on a red, a red only on a black.

(5) *On any suit but its own.* For example, a spade on a heart, diamond or club, but not on another spade.

Any of the following rules may apply regarding rank:

(1) *Up.* A card on a next-lower card. Thus, 'building up in suit' means that a ♦10 goes on a ♦9, etc. 'Building up regardless of suit' means that any ten goes on any nine.

(2) *Down.* A card on a next-higher card. Thus, 'building down in alternate colours' means that a ♥7 goes on either a ♠8 or a ♣8.

(3) *Up, or down, by (a given interval).* For example, building up *by twos* means that a three may be built on an ace, a five on a three, etc., giving the full sequence A, 3, 5, 7, 9, J, K, 2, 4, 6, 8, 10, Q. In every case the text states or illustrates the permissible sequence.

(4) *Either up or down.* A nine either on a ten or an eight, subject to any restriction as to suit. Sometimes, the direction of building may be reversed at will. Sometimes, once begun, it may not be changed. The rule applying to the game in question is always stated in the text.

Build Two or more cards on top of a pile, conforming in suit and sequence to the rules for building on that pile. Usually, where it is permissible to move a build as a single unit, the entire build must be moved, not a portion of it. Sometimes either the top card or the entire build may be moved. When a build is moved as a unit, it is the bottommost card of the build that must fit the card to which the build is moved.

Available card One that may under the rules be moved elsewhere.

In the absence of any rule to the contrary, assume that the available cards are: any card of tableau or reserve not covered in whole or in part by another; the top card of each wastepile; a card newly turned from the stock.

A rule that 'the top of a pile', 'the bottom of a column', etc., is available, means that the removal of such a card makes the next one to it available.

Discard To lay a card aside, out of play for the rest of the game.

Some few games use a 'cut' or 'stripped' pack – one from which certain cards are discarded before dealing begins.

In some full-pack games, cards are discarded during the course of the play. In this event, the object of play is usually to discard all or most of the pack; such games do not usually use foundations.

Redeal Wherever the stock is brought into play one card at a time, unplayable cards being laid in one or more wastepiles, the permission to *redeal* applies only to the wastepiles. That is, the cards of all wastepiles are gathered in a heap and turned face down, forming a new stock which is then turned up one card at a time as before. 'Two redeals are allowed' means that the stock may be run through three times in all, and so on.

In some cases the stock is run through in batches of three, and in all such cases at least two redeals are allowed – the stock may be run through three times. In some cases, the stock may be run through time after time without limit, until the game is won or blocked.

The foundation cards are *never* gathered into the new stock for redealing.

Sometimes tableau cards are gathered for redealing, and in such cases the rules often provide that the new stock be thoroughly shuffled. When only the wastepiles are gathered for redealing, they must not be reshuffled; the order of the cards must not be disturbed.

All exceptions and special conditions are described in full in the text.

Peeking By 'peeking' we mean looking at the next card from the stock before deciding on the next play. Peeking at a face-down card in a reserve or tableau pile is never permitted by the rules; but, as a general rule, this book sanctions peeking at the next card from the stock. Regardless of what is written in the rules, players will follow their own inclinations as to peeking, but in some cases there are special reasons why peeking is not allowed.

Option in play Unless otherwise stated in the rules, the only obligatory plays are of available cards that start foundation piles. Other plays (including builds on foundations) may be made or not as the player chooses, and alternative plays may be taken in any sequence.

The text in many instances rules that 'a space may be filled at once'; in other instances, that 'a space may be kept open'. We recommend that in all other cases the player adopt a specific rule – either a space may be filled at once, or it may be kept open – according to how difficult he wants to make a particular game.

SOLITAIRES
PLAYED WITH
ONE PACK

CANFIELD
(Fascination, Demon, Thirteen)
Time required: 8 minutes
Chance of winning: 1 in 30 games

Layout Deal a pile of 13 cards for the reserve. Since only one card at a time should be exposed, the reserve is best dealt face down and then turned face up after the pile is squared up.

Deal the 14th card above and to the right of the reserve, for the first foundation. Deal a row of four cards to the right of the reserve, forming the tableau.

Canfield layout The ♦8 is the first foundation, and the other eights, as available, will go in a row to its right; the ♠9 tops the reserve pile and the tableau is the row at its right. The ♥10 may be built on ♣J, ♠9 on ♥10, and the next card of the reserve moved into the space left by the ♥10. Customarily, the player holds the stock in his left hand; the wastepile goes below the tableau.

Foundations As the other three cards of the same rank as the first foundation become available, put them in a row with it. Build the foundations up in suit until each pile contains 13 cards. Ranking of cards is continuous, ace above king and below the two.

Tableau building On the tableau piles, build downwards in alternate colours. The top cards are available for play on foundations, but never into spaces, and an entire pile must be moved as a unit for building on another pile. Fill each space at once with the top card of the reserve. After the reserve is exhausted, fill spaces from the wastepile, but at this time a space may be kept open as long as desired.

Play The top of the reserve is always available for play on foundations or tableau.

Turn cards up from the stock in batches of three, being careful not to disturb the order within the batch. The top card of each batch is available, and the lower cards as released by play of the upper. Put the cards as turned on a single wastepile.

Redeal Continue redealing the stock without limit, until the game is blocked or won.

SELECTIVE CANFIELD
This is the same, except that after the reserve is dealt, five cards are dealt in a row beside it. The player may choose any for his first foundation, the other four becoming the tableau.

RAINBOW
Time required: 8 minutes
Chance of winning: 1 in 20 games

Follow all the rules of Canfield except: turn up cards from the stock one at a time. Two redeals are allowed.

JOKER CANFIELD
Time required: 8 minutes
Chance of winning: 1 in 20 games

This is the same as Canfield, but with the joker added to the pack. Whenever the joker becomes available, it must be played on a foundation as a 'wild' card, standing for the next in sequence. Additional cards may be built on the joker. When the natural card becomes available, it is substituted for the joker, which must then be put on top of a foundation pile. If the joker is dealt for the first foundation, call it what you please, naming both rank and suit.

POUNCE

This is Canfield played by two or more players (up to about seven). Each player has his own pack and manipulates his own tableau. (No two packs should be identical in back design.) The foundations are aces, to be moved to the centre as they become available. They are common property, played on by all players alike. The winner of a game is the player who first gets rid of his reserve pile. As in all multiple solitaire games, strict rules of procedure should be devised and enforced to discourage mayhem, e.g. a player may move cards to the foundations only with one hand.

ELEVENS

Time required: 2 minutes
Chance of winning: 1 in 4 games

Deal three rows of three cards each. Discard kings, queens, jacks and tens in quartets of the same rank. Discard lower cards in batches that total 15 – no limitation on the number of cards per batch. Fill spaces from the stock. The game is won if you so discard the entire stock.

FIFTEENS

Time required: 2 minutes
Chance of winning: 1 in 3 games

Deal 16 cards, in four rows of four each. Discard kings, queens, jacks and tens in quartets of the same rank. Discard lower cards in batches that total 15 – no limitation on the number of cards per batch. Fill spaces from the stock. The game is won if you so discard the entire stock.

CHAMELEON

Time required: 8 minutes
Chance of winning: 1 in 30 games

Layout Deal 12 cards in a pile to form the reserve. Keep this pile squared up so that only the top card is visible. Deal the 13th card above the reserve, for the first foundation. Deal three cards in a row to the right of the reserve, forming the tableau.

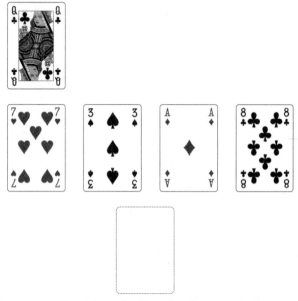

Chameleon layout The ♣Q is the first foundation, and other queens, as available, will go in a row at its right; the ♥7 tops the reserve pile, and the cards at its right are the tableau. The broken lines show the position of the wastepile. The ♥7 may be built on the ♣8.

Foundations Move the other three cards of same rank as the first foundation, as they become available, in a row with it. Build the foundations up in suit until each pile contains 13 cards. Ranking of cards is continuous, ace above king and below the two.

Tableau building On the tableau cards build down regardless of suit. Any or all cards may be lifted off a tableau pile for transfer to another. Fill spaces at once from the top of the reserve. After the reserve is exhausted, fill spaces from the wastepile or stock, as desired.

Play Top cards of the reserve and tableau are always available for building on foundations or tableau. Turn up cards from the stock one at a time, putting unplayable cards in a single wastepile. The top of this pile is always available. There is no redeal.

STOREHOUSE
(Thirteen Up, The Reserve)
Time required: 5 minutes
Chance of winning: 1 in 3 games

Layout Remove the four twos from the pack and put them in a row. Build these foundations up in suit to aces, which rank highest.

Deal 13 cards in a pile at the left, to form the 'storehouse'. To the right of it deal a row of four cards, forming the tableau.

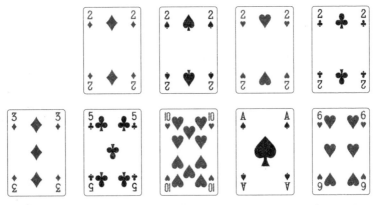

Storehouse layout The ♦3 (top of the reserve pile) may be built on ♦2 in the foundation row; there are no plays in the tableau (row at right of reserve).

Play On the tableau piles, build downwards in suit. Move an entire pile as a unit, for building on another pile. Fill spaces in the tableau at once from the top of the storehouse. After the storehouse is exhausted, fill spaces from the wastepile or stock, as desired.

Top cards of the storehouse, tableau and wastepile are always available for play on foundations or tableau. Turn up cards from the stock one at a time, putting unplayable cards in a single wastepile below the tableau.

Redeals Two redeals are allowed.

30

EAGLE WING
(Thirteen Down)
Time required: 4 minutes
Chance of winning: 1 in 20 games

Layout Deal 13 cards in a pile, face down, forming the 'trunk'. Deal eight cards in a row with the trunk, four on each side, forming the 'wings'. Deal one card in a row above the trunk; this is the first foundation.

Eagle Wing layout The ♠5 is moved up to the foundation row, beside the ♣5, and the top card of the trunk in the centre is turned up to fill the space.

Foundations Move the other cards of same rank as the first foundation, as they become available, into the row with it. Build foundations up in suit until each pile contains 13 cards. The ace (unless it is the foundation) ranks next above the king.

Play Cards in the wings are available for play on the foundations. Fill spaces from the trunk, turning the cards face up in the wings. When only one card remains in the trunk, turn it face up; it may be played directly to a foundation without finding space in the wings first. After the trunk is exhausted, fill spaces from wastepile or stock, as you wish.

Turn up cards from the stock one at a time, putting unplayable cards in a single wastepile. The top of this pile is always available.

Redeals Two redeals are allowed.

31

KLONDIKE
(Canfield, Fascination, Triangle, Demon Patience)
Time required: 8 minutes
Chance of winning: 1 in 30 games

Layout Deal 28 cards in seven piles, with the number of cards per pile increasing from one to seven from left to right; the top card of each pile being face up, the rest face down. The usual method of dealing is by rows – a face-up card, then six face down at its right; a face-up card on top of the second pile, then five face-down at its right, and so on. These 28 cards form the tableau.

Klondike layout The ♣A is moved to the foundation row (shown by dotted lines). The ♠6 may be built on ♦7; ♦K moved into the space left by the ♠6; ♠Q built on ♦K; and the uncovered face-down cards are turned up.

Foundations Move all aces, as they become available, to a row above the tableau. Build them up in suit to kings.

Tableau On the face-up cards in the tableau, build down in alternating colours. The top card of a pile is always available for play on a foundation. All the face-up cards on a pile are moved as a unit when the bottommost of these cards may be built on the top of another pile. (Some players also allow a single card to be moved, even when there are other face-up cards underneath it.)

Whenever the face-up cards of a pile are cleared off, turn up the next card; it becomes available. A space made by clearing away an entire pile may be filled only by a king (plus the cards, if any, built on the king).

Play Turn up cards from the stock one at a time, building them on foundations or tableau. Put unplayable cards in a single wastepile. The top of the wastepile is always available. There is no redeal. (Some players turn up cards from the stock three at a time, facing them in a fan of which the top card is always available, and go through the stock three times in all. Some go through the stock as in Canfield, page 25.)

An ace must be moved into the foundation row as soon as available. But with all other cards you have a choice of building on foundations or leaving the cards in the tableau to help with the manipulation.

JOKER KLONDIKE
Time required: 8 minutes
Chance of winning: 1 in 20 games

This is the same as Klondike, but with the joker added to the pack. Whenever the joker becomes available it must be played on a foundation as a 'wild' card, standing for the next in sequence. Additional cards may be built on the joker. When the natural card becomes available, it is substituted for the joker, which must then be put on top of a foundation pile. If no foundation has been started, it cannot be moved from its position until an ace appears.

KLONDIKE FOR TWO
(Double Solitaire)

Two play, each with his own pack of cards (of different designs or colours). Each manipulates his own tableau, but all foundations form a common pool to which either may play. When the layouts are dealt, the lowest-ranking one-card pile determines the first player; if these cards are of the same rank, then it is the lower of the cards on the two-card piles, and so on. A player's turn ends when he puts a card face up on his wastepile, and his opponent's turn then begins. If a player makes any other play when able to play an ace to a foundation, his turn ends there if his opponent stops him before he has completed a subsequent play. The winner is the player who has played the most cards to the foundations, if and when the game becomes blocked.

MULTIPLE KLONDIKE

This is for two or more players, each playing a game of Klondike simultaneously with the others, and all playing to common foundations. No two packs should be identical in design and colour. A player may be required to play an ace. If two or more try to play identical cards to the same foundation pile, the one who gets it down on the pile has made the play and the other must restore his card to where it came from before he may resume play.

AGNES

Time required: 5 minutes
Chance of winning: 1 in 3 games

Follow all the rules of Klondike except for these modifications: deal the 29th card above the tableau to make the first foundation. Build foundations up in suit, ace ranking between king and two, until each pile contains 13 cards. Below the tableau deal a row of seven cards, forming the reserve. These cards are available for play on foundations and tableau. Whenever play comes to a standstill, deal another row of seven cards on the reserve, forming piles. Do not fill spaces in the reserve except by subsequent deals. Only the top card of a reserve pile is available. Turn the last two cards of the pack face up; both are available.

A space in the tableau may be filled only by a card of rank next-lower to the foundations.

WHITEHEAD

Time required: 8 minutes
Chance of winning: 1 in 20 games

Follow all the rules of Klondike except for these modifications: deal the entire tableau face up, overlapping the cards downwards in column so that all may be inspected. On the tableau, build down in colour (red on red, black on black, regardless of suits). A space may be filled by any available card or build. All cards on top of a tableau pile that are in sequence in the same *suit* may be lifted off as a unit, for transfer to another pile.

34

THUMB AND POUCH
Time required: 5 minutes
Chance of winning: 1 in 4 games

Follow all the rules of Klondike, except for these modifications with regards to building in the tableau. Either the top card of a pile, or all the face-up cards as a unit, may be moved. A card may be built on a card of next-higher rank, of any suit but its own. A space may be filled by any available card or build.

SPIDERETTE
Time required: 8 minutes
Chance of winning: 1 in 20 games

Layout Deal 28 cards in a tableau as for Klondike.

Play There are no foundations; all building is on the tableau. Build down in sequence, ending at ace, regardless of suits (but prefer to build in suit when choice offers). The top card of each pile is available. Cards at the top of a pile that are in correct sequence in the same suit may be lifted as a unit to be built elsewhere. When a face-down card is bared, turn it face up; it becomes available. A space made by removing an entire pile may be filled by any available card or build.

Whenever play comes to a standstill, deal another row of seven cards on the seven piles. Any spaces must be filled prior to the deal. Put the last three cards of the pack on the first three piles.

The object of the play is to get all 13 cards of a suit in correct sequence on top of a pile. Whenever you so assemble a suit, discard it from the tableau. The game is won if you assemble all four suits.

WILL O' THE WISP
Time required: 8 minutes
Chance of winning: 1 in 4 games

This is the same as Spiderette, except that the layout comprises only 21 cards, in seven piles of three cards each, with only the top card of each pile face up.

WESTCLIFF
Time required: 5 minutes
Chance of winning: 9 out of 10 games

Layout Deal 30 cards in a tableau, a row of ten piles of three cards each, with only the top card of each pile face up. The usual way of dealing is by rows, two face down and the last face up.

Westcliff layout The ♣A has been moved to the foundation row and other aces will go beside it. The ♣2 may be built on ♣A, ♠2 or ♦3, ♦6 on ♠7, ♦7 on ♠8, and cards below them turned up.

Foundations Move the aces, as they become available, to a row above the tableau. Build them up in suit to kings.

Tableau building On the tableau, build down in alternating colours. The top of a pile, or all face-up cards as a unit in correct sequence and alternation when the bottommost of such cards is suitable, may be lifted for building on the top of another pile, or to fill a space made by removal of an entire pile. Top cards of the piles are always available for play on foundations. When a face-down card on the tableau is bared, turn it face up; it becomes available.

Play Turn up cards from the stock one at a time, playing them on foundations or tableau. Put unplayed cards in a single wastepile. The top of this pile is always available. There is no redeal.

EASTHAVEN
(Aces Up)
Time required: 5 minutes
Chance of winning: 1 in 4 games

Follow all the rules of Westcliff except for these modifications: deal only seven piles for the tableau, 21 cards in all. A space may be filled only by a king, or build with a king at the bottom. Whenever play comes to a standstill, deal another row of seven cards face up on the tableau. All spaces in the tableau must be filled (if possible) before a new row is dealt. When only three cards remain, put these in a row on the first three tableau piles.

THIRTEENS
(Simple Addition)
Time required: 2 minutes
Chance of winning: 1 in 2 games

Deal two rows of five cards each. Pick out pairs of cards that total 13 and put them in a discard pile: e.g., 8 and 5; jack and 2; queen and ace. Discard kings singly. Fill spaces from the stock. The game is won if you succeed in dealing the entire pack.

PYRAMID
(Pile of Twenty-Eight)
Time required: 4 minutes
Chance of winning: 1 in 50 games

Layout Deal 28 cards in the form of a pyramid (see diagram on next page). This comprises seven rows, the successive rows increasing from one to seven and overlapping so that each card (except in the seventh row) is partly covered by two cards of the next row. At the outset, the seven cards of the last row are available. The removal of any two adjacent cards uncovers one card in the row above. Each card wholly uncovered becomes available.

Play From the available cards, discard pairs of cards that total 13. Discard kings singly. (In the diagram the following may be discarded: ♦K; ♠3 and ♦10; ♣8 and ♥5. Then, with the help of newly-released cards: ♣Q and ♠A; ♦7 and ♥6.)

Turn cards from the stock one at a time, putting unplayable cards in a wastepile. The top of this pile is always available. It may be paired with the next card turned from the stock, or with any released card in the pyramid. There is no redeal.

The game is won if you get all the cards into the discard pile.

PAR PYRAMID
This is a method of scoring Pyramid that establishes degrees of victory. Two redeals are allowed. If you clear the pyramid in one deal, score 50. Then play out the stock cards once to remove any adjacent pairs of cards which total 13, as in the game.

For every card left, deduct one point from your base score of 50. If you clear the pyramid on the second deal, your base score is 35. If you clear it on the third deal, your base score is 20.

'Par' is a net score of zero in six games, and any net plus may be considered a win.

Par Pyramid may be played competitively by two or more, each playing six games with his own pack. The player with the best final net score wins.

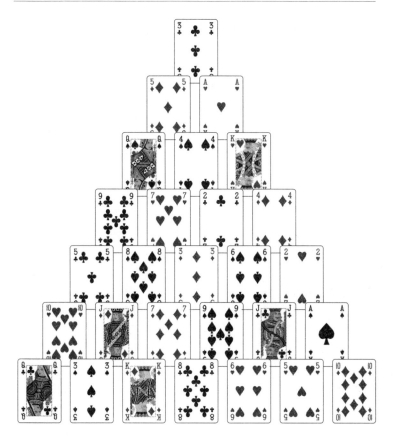

Pyramid layout

BELEAGUERED CASTLE
(Sham Battle, Laying Siege)
Time required: 15 minutes
Chances of winning: 1 in 3 games

Foundations Remove the four aces from the pack and put them in a column. Build these foundations up in suit to kings.

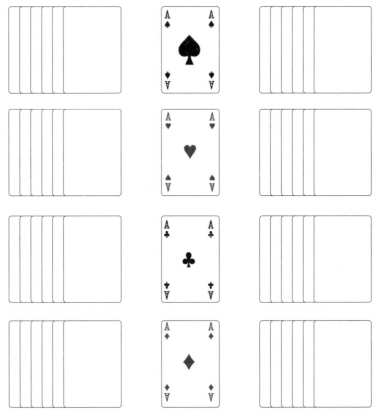

Beleaguered Castle layout The blank outlines represent cards dealt face up.

Tableau Deal the remainder of the pack in two wings of the tableau, one on each side of the aces. Each wing comprises four rows of six cards each. Overlap the cards in each row, so that all are visible but only one at a time is available. The usual method of dealing is by columns, alternately to the left and right wings.

Play On the tableau, build downwards regardless of suit. One card at a time may be lifted from a row and built on a foundation or on the uppermost card of any other row. Only the uppermost card of each row is available. A space made by removing an entire row may be filled by any available card.

Tips Make no move until you have planned a complete line of play that will create a space. If you cannot find a way to do that, the game is probably hopeless. Do not build on foundations merely because you can. Building some foundations ahead of others may cause a block; the higher cards played here may be indispensable for tableau building, to release the lower cards wanted on other foundations. The ideal is to keep all four foundations abreast. It is always safe to play a two or three to a foundation, but thereafter build on foundations only when you can keep them abreast, or when compelled to do so in order to release buried cards.

STREETS AND ALLEYS

Time required: 15 minutes
Chance of winning: 1 in 4 games

This follows the rules of Beleaguered Castle, except that the entire pack is dealt into the tableau. The upper four rows comprise seven cards each, the lower four, six each. Space is left between the rows for the foundations. The aces are moved into the foundations column as they become available.

CITADEL

Time required: 15 minutes
Chance of winning: 1 in 3 games

This is the same as Beleaguered Castle after the deal, but differs in the layout as follows: do not remove aces from the pack, but commence dealing to the tableau (in columns). Whenever you turn an ace, place it in the foundations column instead of on the tableau. Build as you can on the foundations, in the course of dealing, with the proviso that only a newly turned card may be put on a foundation, not a card already on the tableau. Whenever you put a card on a foundation, skip the row where it would have gone on the tableau. The completed rows thus will not be uniform in length.

DECADE
Time required: 2 minutes
Chance of winning: 1 in 50 games

Deal the entire pack in a row, one card at a time. As you go along, toss into the wastepile any two or more adjacent cards that total ten, 20 or 30. Count the kings, queens and jacks as ten each. To win the game you must discard all the cards but one.

FORTRESS
Time required: 15 minutes
Chance of winning: 1 in 10 games

Layout Deal the entire pack in two wings of a tableau (see diagram on next page). Each wing comprises five rows, an upper row of six cards and four rows of five. Overlap the cards in each row so that only one card at a time is available. The usual method of dealing is by columns.

Play Move the four aces, as they become available, to a column between the wings. Build these foundations up in suit to kings. On the tableau, build in suit, either up or down as you please. (You may build up on one row and down on another.) One card at a time – the uppermost card of a row – may be lifted from the tableau to be built on foundations or other tableau rows.

CHESSBOARD
(Fives)
Time required: 15 minutes
Chance of winning: 1 in 5 games

Follow all the rules of Fortress, except that you have your choice of foundations. After dealing the tableau, look it over and decide on the rank of your foundations according to what will best promote manipulation of the tableau.

Fortress layout The blank outlines represent cards dealt face up. The aces, as they become available, will be moved into the spaces indicated by the broken outlines.

SUSPENSE
Time required: 10 minutes
Chance of winning: 1 in 6 games

Layout Deal 24 cards in four groups of six cards each. Form each group as shown in the diagram. The face-down card is the 'centre', the two cards on either side of the centre, in each group, are the 'wings'.

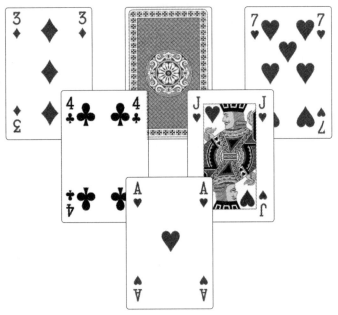

Suspense layout The layout consists of four such groups.

Wastepile Turn up cards from the stock one at a time and put them in a single wastepile. At the beginning of play, the only possible builds are from the layout to the wastepile. On the top card of the wastepile build in sequence up or down regardless of suits. You may change direction as often as you please, it always being permissible to place a card on the next-higher or -lower ranking card. Sequence of rank is continuous, ace being below the two and above the king.

At first, only four cards in the layout are available, the uppermost card of each group. Lower cards become available as the upper are played off to the wastepile.

Foundations The four centre cards are foundations. As each is unburied, move it to a column at the left. Build up in suit on each foundation. Of course, not all four suits will necessarily be represented; in such case, combine foundation piles of the same suit when they are built to the meeting point. Available for foundation-building are: any card of the layout not covered, the top of the wastepile, and a card turned from the stock. It is not compulsory to build when able, but cards on the foundations may not be moved elsewhere.

Tableau Wing cards belong to the tableau. As each is unburied, move it to the right side of the layout. On tableau cards, build down in suit, and combine piles of the same suit when they are built to the meeting point.

A tableau pile may be reversed upon a foundation of the same suit, when the two piles have been built to the meeting point. When the foundations lack one or more suits, these suits must be built up entirely in the tableau.

In the event (very unlikely) that one or more suits are entirely missing from the foundations and wing cards, all cards of those suits may be discarded from the pack as soon as the fact is discovered. (Discard them in dealing, as they turn up in the stock.)

A wing card may be built on the wastepile, provided that another card of the same suit is visible at that time among the foundation or tableau cards. Such sacrifice of a wing card is in general poor policy, but might be necessary to uncover quickly some cards still buried in the layout.

Redeals Two redeals are allowed. You win the game when all cards are built on foundations or tableau.

Tips Don't worry about the direction of builds in the wastepile. Uncover wing and foundation cards as fast as possible, without sacrificing wing cards. Normally, the layout should be completely dissolved well before the end of the first deal. Don't overlook opportunities to play from the layout to such foundations and tableau cards as you have uncovered; such moves are of course preferable to loading the wastepile.

FLOWER GARDEN
(The Garden, Bouquet)
Time required: 15 minutes
Chance of winning: 1 in 2 games

Layout Deal a 'garden' (tableau) of 36 cards in six rows of six. Overlap the rows, forming six piles spread downwards. Spread the remaining 16 cards below the garden to form the 'bouquet' (reserve).

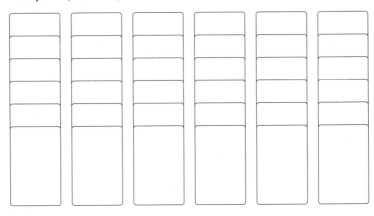

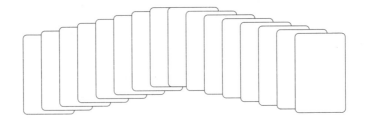

Flower Garden layout The piles of cards above are the tableau; the fan of cards below is the reserve. All cards are dealt face up.

Foundations Move the four aces, as they become available, to a row above the garden. Build them up in suit to kings.

Play On the columns of the garden, build down regardless of suits. One card at a time may be lifted from the top of a pile and played on a foundation or on the top card of another pile. A space made by removing a whole column of the garden may be filled by any available card. Every card of the bouquet is available at all times for play on foundations or garden.

Tips Do not use bouquet cards for building in the garden if avoidable, for to do so permanently decreases the number of cards available at one time. For the same reason, a space is not an unmixed blessing. Loading up the other columns to make a space may prove too costly. Aim primarily to release all the aces, twos and threes, for the immolation of a single low card may block the game.

KING ALBERT
Time required: 15 minutes
Chance of winning: 1 in 2 games

Layout Deal 45 cards in a tableau of nine piles of overlapping cards, spread downward, the number of cards per pile increasing from one to nine. It is easiest to lay by rows.

Below this tableau spread the remaining seven cards of the pack, forming the reserve.

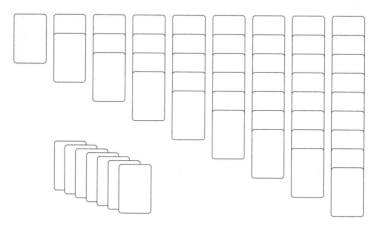

King Albert layout All cards are dealt face up.

Foundations Move the four aces, as they become available, to a row above the tableau. Build them up in suit to kings.

Play On the tableau piles, build down in alternate colours. One card at a time may be lifted from the top of a pile to be built on foundations or on the top card of another pile. A space made by removing an entire pile may be filled by any available card. All cards of the reserve are available for play on foundations or tableau.

YUKON
Time required: 8 minutes
Chance of winning: 1 in 4 games

Layout Deal 28 cards in seven piles, as for Klondike (see page 32). Deal the remaining 24 cards evenly upon the six piles other than the single card. Overlap all the face-up cards downwards, so that all may be seen.

Foundations Move the four aces, as they become available, to a row above the tableau. Build them up in suit to kings.

Play On the top card of a tableau pile may be built a next-lower card of opposite colour, except that no build may be made on an ace. An ace at the top of a pile must be moved at once to the foundation row, but it is not compulsory to build higher cards on the foundations; such cards may be kept in the tableau for building.

Any card in the tableau, no matter how deeply buried, may be moved to make a build; all the cards covering it are moved with it as a unit.

On clearing a face-down card, turn it face up; it then becomes available. Top cards of all piles are available for building on foundations.

A space made by clearing away an entire pile may be filled only by a king. For this purpose any king in sight is available, all covering cards being moved with it as a unit.

Tips Aim first of all to uncover the face-down cards. Build on foundations only as an aid to manipulating the tableau. Be wary of building any foundation far ahead of another, lest cards vital for building be put out of reach.

LA BELLE LUCIE
(The Fan, Clover Leaf, Midnight Oil, Alexander the Great)
Time required: 15 minutes
Chance of winning: 1 in 10 games

Layout Deal the whole pack in 17 fans (piles spread so that all cards are visible) of three cards each. The card left over forms a separate pile.

La Belle Lucie layout All cards are dealt face up.

Foundations Move the four aces, as they become available, to a row near you. Build these foundations up in suit to kings.

Play On the tableau fans, build down in suit. One card at a time may be lifted from a fan to be put on a foundation or another fan. Spaces made by playing off a whole fan are not filled.

Redeals Two redeals are allowed. After play has come to a standstill, gather all the cards not on the foundations, shuffle them and deal again in fans of three. If one or two cards are left over, they make a separate fan.

Draw. After the last redeal, any one buried card may be drawn out of any one fan.

Tips Once a build is made, it cannot be unmade except by play on a foundation. Therefore make no build until you have assured yourself that: (a) the cards below, thereby immolated, are not needed, or cannot be released anyhow; or (b) the build is sure to find eventual place on a foundation; or (c) burying the cards beyond recovery, to release others, is a worthwhile investment.

One way to begin, after the deal, is to note all the cards buried by kings. Since the cards next-lower in sequence to these buried cards cannot be moved, they can be built upon without further ado. For example, if the ♠10 is below a king, build on the ♠9. Similarly, having immolated some cards by a build, proceed to build freely on the cards next-lower in suit.

The layout usually offers many choices of play. Canvass all possibilities before making a move. For example, suppose that ♣4, 5 and 6 are available. If the ♣5 and ♣4 are built on the ♣6, that fan is killed. If the ♣4 is first built on the ♣5, that pile is killed, while the ♣6 can perhaps be moved later through clearing the ♣7. The choice of play will of course depend on whether the cards below the ♣5 or below the ♣6 are wanted more urgently.

Play on foundations at every opportunity, since if a card is playable on a foundation it is of no use in the tableau.

TREFOIL

This is the same as La Belle Lucie, except that the four aces are removed from the pack in advance and put in the foundation row. The first tableau comprises 16 fans of three.

SHAMROCKS
(Three-card Fan)
Time required: 15 minutes
Chance of winning: 1 in 4 games

Layout Deal the whole pack in 17 fans of three cards each, with one card left over. (See diagram of La Belle Lucie, page 49.) If you find any king above another card of the same suit, transfer it below that card.

Foundations Move the four aces, as they become available, for a foundation row. Build them up in suit to kings.

Play On the tableau fans, build in sequence, up or down as you wish, regardless of suits. (You may build both ways on the same pile.) But no fan may comprise more than three cards. One card at a time may be lifted off a fan, for play on foundations or another fan. A space made by playing off an entire fan is never filled.

Tips The layout is a block if you do not find an ace on top of one of the fans and if no available card can be built upon the single card. It is suggested that in such case, to save redealing, you draw out one of the buried ones.

Do not build on foundations merely because you can – you may thereby deprive the tableau of cards vital for building. The ideal way to avoid this self-made block is to keep the four foundations abreast.

Once a fan is gone, you have one less pile for building. Never move the last card of a fan on to another fan, and play it to a foundation only when the move is perfectly safe (the foundations are abreast) or urgently necessary (to break an impasse).

STALACTITES
(Old Mole, Grampus)
Time required: 8 minutes
Chance of winning: 5 out of 6 games

Layout Deal a row of four cards for foundations. Turn these cards sidewise, so that when cards are built on them in the normal way the base cards will always be identifiable.

Below the foundations, deal the rest of the pack in a tableau of six rows of eight cards each, the cards overlapping to form eight piles spread downward.

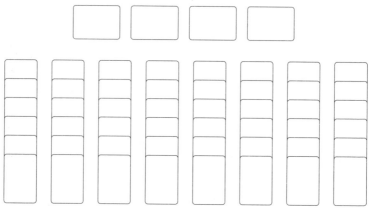

Stalactites layout All cards are dealt face up, the foundations in the row of horizontal cards above, the tableau piles below. Cards played on the foundations will be placed in normal (vertical) position.

Foundations Inspect the layout and decide whether to build the foundations by ones or twos, e.g. 7, 8, 9, 10, J or 7, 9, J, K, 2, 4, etc. The decision applies to all four foundations. Build them up by the chosen interval, ignoring suits, until each pile contains 13 cards. (The visible base card warns you when to stop.)

Play Only the top card of each pile is available, but two cards may be removed from anywhere in the tableau and held out in a reserve, with the proviso that the reserve may never comprise more than two cards. The reserve cards are also available for building on foundations. Spaces made by removal of an entire tableau column are never filled.

AULD LANG SYNE
(Patience)
Time required: 2 minutes
Chance of winning: 1 in 100 games

Layout Remove the four aces from the pack and put them in a row. These are foundations, to be built up to kings regardless of suits.

Auld Lang Syne layout There is no available play from the reserve (lower row) to the foundations, so another reserve row must be dealt on the first.

Play Deal the stock into four reserve piles, one row of four cards at a time. After dealing each batch of four, play up what you can from the tops of the reserve piles on to the foundations. Cards in the reserve piles become available when they are uncovered, but may not be used to fill spaces. There is no redeal.

HIT OR MISS
(Treize, Roll Call, Talkative, Harvest)
Time required: 15 minutes
Chance of winning: 1 in 50 games

Deal cards one at a time into one pile, called 'Ace' for the first card, 'Two' for the second, and so on. After 'King', call the next card 'Ace', and so through the pack.

When a card proves to be of the rank you call, it is *hit*. Discard all hit cards from the pack. The object of play is to hit every card in the pack – eventually.

Whenever the stock is exhausted, turn over the wastepile to form a new stock, and continue counting from where you left off. The game is construed lost if you go through the stock twice in succession without a hit. (The point of this rule is that unlimited redealing would surely win the game unless a no-hit were encountered when the stock comprises 52, 39, 26 or 13 cards.)

OLD PATIENCE
(Try Again, Sir Tommy)
Time required: 5 minutes
Chance of winning: 1 in 5 games

Foundations Move the four aces, as they become available, into a row. Build each ace up to king, regardless of suits.

Play Turn up cards from the stock one at a time, placing each on any of four wastepiles. After each batch of four cards, pause and play up what you can from the wastepiles to the foundations. Only the top card of each pile is available.

Tips When placing a card on a wastepile, prefer to place it on a higher card than a lower card. When this policy is not feasible, place a card on a pile that does not contain a card of the same rank. But this rule has its exceptions: most vital of all is to avoid burying all four cards of one rank under higher cards.

PUSS IN CORNER
Time required: 10 minutes
Chance of winning: 1 in 3 games

Foundations Remove the four aces from the pack and put them in a square. These are foundations, to be built up in colour to kings. (Red on red, black on black, otherwise regardless of suits.)

Puss in Corner layout The ♣2 may be built on either the ♣A or the ♠A.

Play Turn up cards from the stock one at a time, placing them on any of four wastepiles. (These piles are traditionally placed at the four corners of the foundation-square, thus giving the game its name.) After each batch of four cards, pause and play up what you can from the piles to the foundations. Only the top card of each pile is available.

Redeal One redeal is allowed. Pick up the wastepiles in any prefixed order, as clockwise from the lower left corner.

Tips See Old Patience (page 54).

FOUR SEASONS
(Corner Card, Vanishing Cross)
Time required: 5 minutes
Chance of winning: 1 in 10 games

Layout Deal a tableau of five cards in the form of a cross. Deal the sixth card in one corner of the cross, forming the first foundation.

Four Seasons layout The ♣J is the first foundation; the other cards are the tableau. The ♦5 may be built on the ♥6.

Foundations Put the other three cards of same rank as the first foundation, when they become available, in the remaining corners of the cross. Build the foundations up in suit (ace ranking next above king) until each pile contains 13 cards.

Tableau building Build down regardless of suit; a king may be played on an ace, unless aces are foundations. One card at a time may be moved from the top of a pile elsewhere. Fill spaces with any available cards from tableau, wastepile or stock.

Play Turn cards from stock one at a time, playing them on foundations or tableau. Put unplayable cards in a single wastepile. The top of this pile is always available.

SIMPLICITY
Time required: 5 minutes
Chances of winning: 9 out of 10 games

This is the same as Four Seasons except: the tableau is two rows of six cards each. Deal the 13th card for the first foundation. On the tableau, build down in alternating colours.

ACCORDION
(Idle Year, Tower of Babel, Methuselah)
Time required: 5 minutes
Chance of winning: 1 in 100 games

Deal the entire pack in a row, one card at a time. A card may be moved upon its left-hand neighbour, or upon the card third to its left, if the two cards concerned are of the same suit or rank. A pile of two or more cards is moved as a unit, the legality of the move depending on its top card. The game is won if you get the entire pack into one pile.

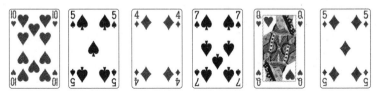

Accordion layout The ♦5 may be moved on to ♦4, then both on ♠5, then ♥Q on ♥10.

Tips With choice of plays, before making any play, deal a few more cards to see if there is a choice.

BAKER'S DOZEN

Time required: 15 minutes
Chances of winning: 2 out of 3 games

Layout Deal the entire pack in four rows of 13 cards each, overlapping the rows to form piles of cards spread downwards. Then transfer every king to the bottom of its pile.

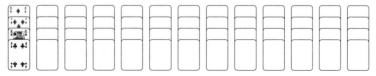

Baker's Dozen layout The ♠K will be put under the ♦3. All the outlines represent other face-up cards.

Foundations Move the four aces, as they become available, to a row above the tableau. Build them up in suit to kings.

Play One card at a time may be lifted from the top of a pile and built on a foundation or on the top card of another pile. On the tableau, build down regardless of suit. A space made by removing a whole pile may not be filled.

Tips Note every card lying over (in sense of availability) a lower card of the same suit. Whether or not any cards intervene between the two, this situation is a reversal that must be resolved by tableau building. Aim primarily to straighten out all such 'kinks'. Be wary of building one foundation ahead of another; a block may result for lack of a builder moved prematurely to a foundation.

GOOD MEASURE

Time required: 15 minutes
Chance of winning: 2 out of 3 games

This follows all the rules of Baker's Dozen, except that the first two aces turned up in dealing are put at once into the foundation row instead of the tableau, and the latter is dealt in five rows, making ten spread piles of five cards each.

58

LITTLE SPIDER
Time required: 20 minutes
Chance of winning: 2 out of 3 games

Layout Deal the whole pack into eight piles, dealt as two rows of four with room between for a row of foundations. All cards are dealt face up. After dealing each batch of eight cards, one to each pile, pause and play what you can on the foundations. The last four cards of the pack go on the top row.

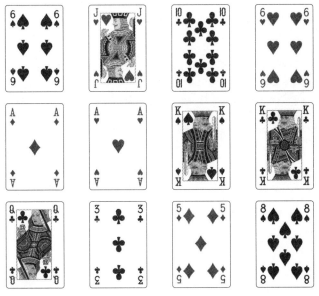

Little Spider layout The cards in the top and bottom rows are the tops of tableau piles; the cards in the middle row are the foundations.

Foundations Move the two aces of one colour, and the two kings of the other colour, as they turn up during the deal, into the foundation row. You can choose red aces and black kings or black aces and red kings, as you wish. Build the aces up in suit to kings and the kings down in suit to aces.

59

Play During the deal, a foundation ace or king may be moved into place from either the upper or lower row of the tableau. From the upper row, playable cards may be transferred to any foundations. From a tableau pile of the lower row, however, an additional card may be played up only to the foundation directly above it.

After the deal is complete, the top card of every pile is available for play on all foundations and all other piles. On the tableau, build in sequence up or down as you please, regardless of suits. The sequence here is continuous, the ace ranking below the two and above the king. A space made by removing an entire pile may not be filled.

Tips Don't hurry to build up the foundations; save cards as long as possible for tableau building. Try to bring together cards of the same suit, built in sequence opposite from the direction of the foundation of that suit, so that in due time they can all be skimmed off.

ROYAL FLUSH
Time required: 2 minutes
Chance of winning: 1 in 5 games

As in poker, the royal flush is A K Q J 10 of the same suit.

Deal the entire pack into a row of five piles, face down, putting the two extra cards on the first two piles.

Turn over the first pile and discard its cards one by one (if necessary) until any card of rank ten or higher appears. This card fixes the suit of the royal flush. For example, if the first card of sufficient rank is ♥10, the royal flush will be ♥A K Q J 10. If no high card shows in the first pile, go on to the second pile, etc., until one shows.

With the suit fixed, turn over the next pile and discard its cards until you reach a card of the royal flush; then do the same with each remaining pile. When a pile contains no flush card, discard it. (It may be easier to fan out the piles, face up, and discard all cards that lie above any card of the flush.)

Turn the piles face down and gather them into a new stock, reversing the order in which they were dealt before – putting each pile on the one at its left. Deal the new stock into four piles, as far as the cards will go. Turn them over (or fan them) again, and discard all cards on top of the royal flush cards as before. Reversing the order again, gather them into a new stock, face down, and deal three piles; again turn the piles face up and discard down to the royal flush cards. Gather them, reversing the order again, deal two piles, and discard as before.

The game is won if now only the five cards of the royal flush remain, and no other.

ROYAL MARRIAGE
(Betrothal, Matrimony, Coquette)
Time required: 4 minutes
Chance of winning: 1 in 2 games

Put the ♥K on the bottom of the pack, and the ♥Q on the table at your left. Deal the entire pack in a row with the ♥Q, one card at a time. As you go along, discard any one card or any two adjacent cards that are enclosed by two cards of the same suit or rank. The game is won if you get the royal couple, ♥K and ♥Q, side by side.

CLOCK
(Hidden Cards, Four of a Kind, Travellers, Sun Dial)
Time required: 3 minutes
Chance of winning: 1 in 100 games

Layout Deal the pack into 13 piles of four cards each, face down. Traditionally, the piles should be arranged like a clock dial – 12 piles in a circle, the 13th in the centre. In any event, the piles must regarded as being numbered from one to 13.

Play Turn up the top card of the 13th pile (centre of the clock face). Put it face up under the pile of its own number, jack counting as 11, queen as 12, king as 13, ace as 1. For example, if it is the ♣6 put it under the sixth pile, the pile at 'six o'clock'. Turn up the top of the sixth pile and put it under the pile of its own number. Continue in this way, putting a card under a pile and then turning up the top card of that pile. If the last face-down card of the any pile belongs to that pile, turn next the face-down card of the next pile clockwise around the circle.

The game is won if all 13 piles become changed into fours-of-a-kind. It is lost if the fourth king is turned up before all other fours are completed.

WATCH
Time required: 3 minutes
Chance of winning: 1 in 20 games

Follow all the rules of Clock, but if you are blocked before the game is won, draw any one face-down card, exchange it for the king just turned and continue play. If the king again turns up before all the other fours are completed, the game is lost.

GRANDFATHER'S CLOCK
Time required: 8 minutes
Chance of winning: 3 out of 4 games

Foundations Take from the pack the following 12 cards: ♥2, ♠3, ♦4, ♣5, ♥6, ♠7, ♦8, ♣9, ♥10, ♠J, ♦Q, ♣K. Put them in a circle corresponding to the hours on a clock dial, with the ♣9 at '12 o'clock' and the rest in sequence around the circle.

Grandfather's Clock layout All cards are dealt face up.

Build each foundation up in suit until it reaches the number appropriate to its position on the clock. Jack represents 11, queen 12, king 13, and ace 1. The sequence of rank is continuous, with ace below two and above king. The 10, J, Q and K foundations will each require the addition of four cards; all others will take three cards.

Tableau Deal the rest of the pack into five rows of eight cards each. Overlap the rows to form piles of cards spread downwards.

Play The top card of each tableau pile is available for play on a foundation or on the top card of another pile. On the tableau, build down regardless of suit. A space made by playing off a whole pile may be filled by any available card.

RONDO
(Eight-day Clock, Perpetual Motion)
Time required: 20 minutes
Chance of winning: 1 in 20 games

Layout Deal the pack into 13 piles of four cards each, face up. The piles must be construed as numbered from one to 13. Arrange them in whatever array you find most helpful in keeping track of the numbers.

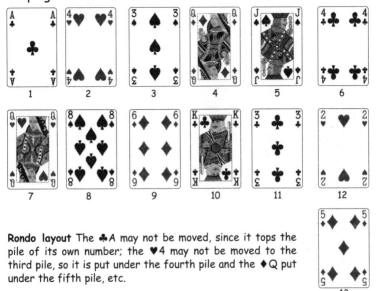

Rondo layout The ♣A may not be moved, since it tops the pile of its own number; the ♥4 may not be moved to the third pile, so it is put under the fourth pile and the ♦Q put under the fifth pile, etc.

Play The whole play consists of 'weaving'. Move the top card of pile 1 below pile 2; the top card of pile 2 below pile 3; and so on around the circuit. From pile 13 return to pile 1. But when a pile is topped by a card of its own number (counting jack 11, queen 12, king 13, ace 1) you can neither move its top card nor put a card under it; you skip that pile and go to the next available pile beyond.

The effect of the transfer is (usually) to bring more and more cards to the tops of like-numbered piles, so decreasing the circuit of piles included in the transfers. When finally each of the 13 piles is topped by a card of its own number, lift off and discard these 13 top cards.

The last card removed before this happy event has for the moment 'nowhere to go'. Lay it aside until the 13 top cards are discarded. Then resume play by putting it under the pile of its own number (or the first thereafter which is available under the rule).

Continue play in the same way; the game is won if you discard three sets of 13 cards.

PERPETUAL MOTION
Time required: 60 minutes
Chance of winning: 1 in 4 games

Deal a row of four cards. If two or three are of the same rank, move the others upon the leftmost of the equal cards. Deal another row of four upon the first. Move cards if you can, so as to being equal cards together leftwards. Continue dealing the pack in batches of four, making what plays you can after each deal. If all four cards dealt in a row are of the same rank, discard them and deal another row.

After you have run through the pack, put the rightmost pile on its left neighbour; put this augmented pile on the one at the left, and then the triple pile on the leftmost. Turn the cards face down to form a new stock, and continue play as before. Be careful not to shuffle, or let the cards become disarranged, once the game has begun. Redeal without limit, until the game is decided.

Each time you deal a row of four cards that prove to be all of the same rank, discard these four cards from the pack. The game is won if you eventually discard the entire pack in batches of four.

When the pack is reduced to 12 or eight cards, fan it out before the first deal and observe the order of the cards. If this identical order recurs at some later time, resign the game.

OSMOSIS
(Treasure Trove)
Time required: 5 minutes
Chance of winning: 1 in 8 games

Layout Deal four piles of four cards each, in a column at the left. Since only the top card of each pile should be known, the cards are best dealt face down and then turned face up after the packets are squared up.

Foundations Deal one card at the right of the top reserve pile. This is the first foundation. Put the other cards of same rank, as they become available, in a column below the first.

Build each foundation in suit, regardless of order. Put the cards in a row with the foundation, overlapping, so that all are visible. On the first foundation, any card of the same suit may be built as soon as it becomes available. On each lower formation, a card may be built only if a card of the same rank has been built on the foundation above. For example, suppose that the first foundation is the ♦J, and the second is the ♠J. Finding the ♦7, 4, K available, you have piled them on the ♦J. You may continue putting any diamonds on the foundation, but at the moment the only spades you may put on the ♠J are the ♠4, 7, K.

Play Top cards of the reserve piles are available for play on foundations. Turn up cards from the stock in batches of three. Do not disturb the order of the cards in counting off these batches. The top card of the batch is available, also the lower cards if released by play of the upper. Put each residue of unplayable cards in a single wastepile. Redeal without limit until the game is blocked, or is won by getting the entire pack on to the foundations.

PEEK

Follow the rules of Osmosis, but spread the reserve piles so that all cards may be seen. Sight of the entire reserve often curtails play by revealing a hopeless block. Sometimes it enables a block to be avoided by withholding one foundation card until another becomes available.

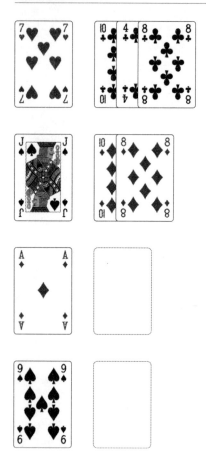

Osmosis after several plays Any club, when it becomes available, may be played to the top foundation row (on the ♣8); only the ♦4 could be played at this point, to the second foundation row; the ♠10 or the ♥10 could be played to the third foundation row (indicated by broken lines below the ♦10 and ♦8).

SCORPION

Time required: 8 minutes
Chance of winning: 1 in 10 games

Layout Deal seven cards in a row, four face down and three face up. Deal two more rows in the same way; then four more rows with all the cards face up. Overlap the rows to form piles of cards spread downward.

The 49 cards so dealt make the tableau. Leave the three remaining cards face down, as a reserve.

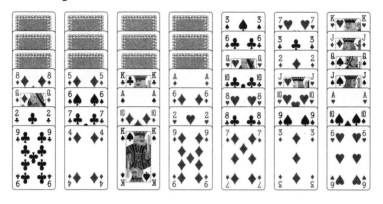

Scorpion layout The ♦8, ♦Q, ♣2 and ♣9 may be moved as a unit to the ♦9, and the card below the ♦8 turned up; the ♦3 may be moved to the ♦4; etc.

Play All building is confined to the tableau, there being no separate foundations. The object of play is to reduce the tableau to four piles, one of each suit, with the cards of each suit in sequence, the king at the bottom of the pile.

On the top card of each pile may be placed the next-lower card of the same suit; nothing may be built on an ace. Any card in the tableau, no matter how deeply buried, may be moved to make a build; but all the cards above it must be moved with it as a unit.

On clearing a face-down card, turn it face up; it then becomes available.

A space made by clearing away an entire pile may be filled only by a king. Any king in sight is available for this purpose, all covering cards being moved with it as a unit.

Reserve After play comes to a standstill, deal the three reserve cards, one on top of each of the three leftmost piles. Resume play; if the game again becomes blocked, it is lost.

Tips Look at each face-up card that covers a face-down card. Trace backwards to see if it can be removed. For example, suppose one of such cards is the ♦8. Look for the ♦9. If you find it, note the card that covers it, say the ♣Q. Look for the ♣K – and so on. The first objective is to make a series of moves that will uncover face-down cards. Often there is a choice regarding which way to 'break' two piles – as, the second pile on the fourth, or the fourth on the second. Some builds will preclude others. All such choices should be made primarily to get at the buried cards.

Similarly, when you have a space, trace the series of plays that would follow; the proper choice of king may create another space.

You do not have to fill the spaces before dealing the reserve cards. With no positive advantage in sight from using a space – such as uncovering a buried card or making another space – hold the first space until you see the reserve cards. For this purpose, manoeuvre to keep a space among the four piles at the right, not among the three at the left.

The game will inevitably become blocked if the tableau contains a 'reversed sequence' or a 'criss-cross' – for example, ♠Q, J or K, adjacent in that order down a pile; or ♣10 directly on ♥4 and ♥3 directly on ♣J. Careless play may create an impasse where none existed before. Suppose that the end cards of two piles (reading down) are ♦4 and ♦6 (on one pile) and ♦5 and ♦3 (on the other). To build the ♦3 on the ♦4 will make a block. The right way is to build the ♦4 on the ♦5, then the ♦5 on the ♦6, then the ♦3 on the ♦4.

MOOJUB
Time required: 4 minutes
Chance of winning: 1 in 2 games

Layout Deal a column of four cards at the left, forming a reserve.

Foundations The number of foundation cards depends upon chance – the more such cards, the better the chance of winning the game. The foundations must be put in columns to the right of the reserve.

At the top of the first foundation column, put the lowest-ranking card that shows in the reserve. Below it must go the lowest-ranking available card of a *different* suit; below that a third suit, and below that the fourth, forming the first foundation column of four cards of different suits, each card being the lowest of its suit available at that time. (Ace is ranked low, under the two.)

The first foundation column fixes the suits; thereafter, each foundation column must be formed of the four suits in the same order.

On every foundation card, build up in suit with the ranking of cards continuous, ace above king and below the two.

Play Continue dealing the stock in batches of four, one card on each reserve pile. The top card of each pile is available. Whenever an available card can be built on a foundation pile, it must be so built. When no build is possible, available cards may be placed in position as new foundation cards, always provided that:

(1) Each foundation column must comprise cards of all four suits before a new column may be started; and foundation cards must be put out in order from top to bottom;

(2) Each new foundation card must be of the same suit as the card at its left;

(3) With choice of available cards to make a new foundation, the lowest of the suit must be taken.

A space in the reserve is never filled except by the subsequent deal of four cards.

The game is won if, after the stock is exhausted, all the cards have been placed into the foundation rows.

Moojub after several plays
The column at the extreme left is the reserve; all other cards are foundations. The ♣6 may be played beside the ♣3; then the ♣7 on the ♣6; then the ♠A beside the ♠5. If these plays have uncovered a heart, the lowest such heart (other than the ♥3 or ♥A) may be played as a new foundation beside the ♥K.

BLOCK ELEVEN
(Calling Out)
Time required: 1 minute
Chance of winning: 1 in 5 games

Deal 12 cards, in three rows of four each. If any kings, queens or jacks show in this layout, remove them and place them on the bottom of the stock. Deal from the top to fill up the layout, moving any additional face cards that turn up to the bottom of the pack, until the layout shows 12 lower cards.

If no face card shows in the original layout, place the first face card turned up in play on the bottom of the pack (for without a face card at the bottom the game cannot be won).

With the layout complete (all non-face cards), begin play. Deal cards from the stock on each pair of cards that total 11. When a face card is dealt, it blocks further play on that pile. The game is won if you succeed in running through the pack, ending with the 12 face cards covering the tableau.

GAPS
Time required: 10 minutes
Chance of winning: 1 in 20 games

Layout Deal the whole pack in four rows of 13 cards each (not overlapped). Then discard the aces, creating four gaps.

Play Into each gap move the card next-higher in suit to the card at the left of the gap. As the sequence ends with a king, so no card may be moved into a gap to the right of a king. Fill each gap at the extreme left of a row with a two. To win the game you must get one entire suit on each row, in proper sequence with the two.

Redeal Continue filling gaps as they are created, until all are blocked by kings. Then gather all the cards not in proper suit and sequence with twos at the left ends of rows. Shuffle them and redeal so as to fill out each row to 13, including a gap left just to the right of the cards already in proper sequence. Two such redeals are allowed.

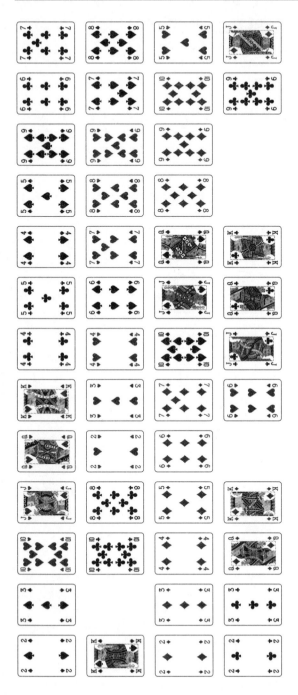

Gaps after several plays Each gap is blocked by a king. Now all cards in the top row at the right of the ♠3; the entire second row; all cards in the third row to the right of the ♦7, and all cards in the bottom row to the right of the ♣3, should be gathered up, shuffled and redealt. In the top row, the first such card will be dealt in the space formerly occupied by the ♥J; in the second row, in the space beside the ♠K; in the third row, in the space of the ♠J, and in the bottom row in the space of the ♦K. Play will then be resumed as before.

74

BISLEY
Time required: 5 minutes
Chance of winning: 2 out of 3 games

Foundations Remove the four aces from the pack and put them in a row at the extreme left. Put the four kings, as they become available, in a row above the aces. Build the aces up in suit, and the kings down in suit. (It does not matter where two foundations of the same suit meet, so long as the entire suit is built on them.)

Tableau Deal nine cards in a row to the right of the aces, then deal the rest of the pack in three more rows of 13 cards each, below the first.

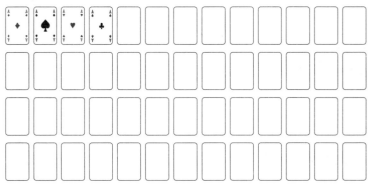

Play The bottom card of each column is available for play on a foundation or on the bottom card of another column. On bottom cards of the tableau, build in suit either up or down, as you wish. An ace may be built only on a two, a king only on a queen. A space made by removing an entire column may not be filled.

Tips Build on foundations at every opportunity – no hazard is incurred in doing so. The risk comes in building down on a column in which a lower card of the same suit is buried. For example, if a ♠6 is built on a five, the ♠9 being in the column, this build obviously cannot be built on a foundation. It will, therefore, have to be reversed eventually on the ♠7, to reach the ♠9. Since such building is often unavoidable, earmark the cards that definitely must be saved in the tableau.

PENDULUM
Time required: 30 minutes
Chance of winning: 1 in 30 games

Foundations Remove the four aces from the pack and put them in a column at the right. Build them up in suit by any interval you choose, after examining the tableau. (For example, if you elect to build up by fives, the sequence is: A, 6, J, 3, 8, K, 5, 10, 2, 7, Q, 4, 9.) You may chose to build consecutively (A, 2, 3, etc.). The chosen interval applies to all four foundations.

Tableau Deal the rest of the pack into six rows of eight cards each (not overlapping).

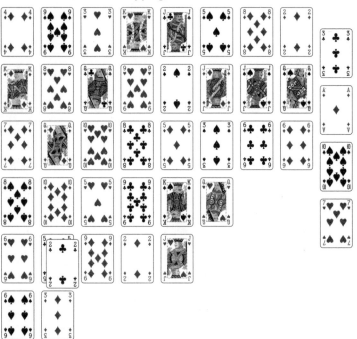

Pendulum after several plays The pendulum has just been swung to the left. The building is by threes; note that the ♣2 has been built on the ♣5. The ♣6 may now be played on the ♣3; then, there being no further plays, the pendulum must be swung back to the right again.

Play The bottom card of each tableau column is available for play on foundations. In addition, it may be built upon the card immediately above it in its column, if that card is of the same suit and next-higher in the selection foundation-sequence. (For example, if the interval is up by fives, the ♥2 may be built on the ♥7.) A build of two or more cards at the bottom of a column may be moved from the next card above, if the suit and sequence are correct. A card from the bottom of any column may be built upon either of the two cards at the upper corners of the tableau, suit and sequence being correct.

A space made by removing an entire column may be filled only by a card, if available, that is of the last rank called for on the foundations. For example, if the selected interval is up by fives, only nines may go into spaces. It is obligatory to fill a space as soon as possible.

The pendulum Whenever play comes to a standstill, 'swing the pendulum'. The first swing must be to the right, and thereafter to the left and right alternately. The swing is accomplished by moving the cards in rows that contain gaps (except the top row) towards one side of the tableau, leaving all the gaps on the opposite side. Do not change the order of the cards within the row.

By changing the position of the cards in lower rows, the swing makes new cards available. The pendulum may be swung repeatedly, without limit, until the game is won or becomes blocked.

FIVE PILES
(Thirteens, Baroness)
Time required: 3 minutes
Chance of winning: 1 in 5 games

Deal a row of five cards. Discard each pair of cards that total 13; as 8 and 5; jack and 2; queen and ace. Discard kings singly. Continue dealing by fives from the stock, one card on each pile, and discard what you can. Only the top card of each pile is available. The last two cards of the pack are spread separately from the tableau and both are available. The game is won if you cast out the whole pack in 13s.

CALCULATION
(Broken Intervals)
Time required: 15 minutes
Chance of winning: 1 in 5 games

Foundations Remove from the pack any ace, two, three and four. Place them in a row. These foundations are to be built up as follows, regardless of suits:

A, 2, 3, 4, 5, 6, 7, 8, 9, 10, J, Q, K
2, 4, 6, 8, 10, Q, A, 3, 5, 7, 9, J, K
3, 6, 9, Q, 2, 5, 8, J, A, 4, 7, 10, K
4, 8, Q, 3, 7, J, 2, 6, 10, A, 5, 9, K

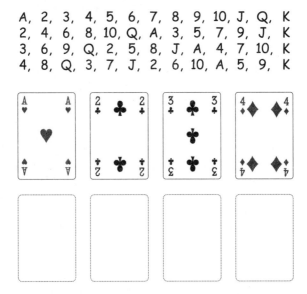

Calculation layout Any two may be played on the ♥A, any four on the ♣2, any six on the ♣3 and any eight on the ♦4; unplayable cards may be placed in any of the positions indicated by the broken lines.

Play Turn up cards from the stock one at a time, placing each either on a foundation or on any one of four wastepiles. These piles are best kept spread downwards, so that all cards may be seen. Only the top of each pile is available. Cards may be moved up to foundations at any time.

Tips As a rule, one wastepile has to be earmarked for kings. To lay a king on any lower card is hazardous, since it can be removed only by building up one foundation complete. But when three kings, possibly two, have been laid in the reserve, it may be advisable to use all four piles for lower cards and chance that the remaining kings will not come too soon.

The natural policy is to try to build descending sequences on the wastepiles, corresponding to the foundation sequences. Of course, the cards are rarely so kind as to allow these builds to be extended very far, but a judicious scattering of sequences of two to four cards works wonders.

As a rule, avoid laying a card on a pile that contains another of the same rank, but this rule may well be ignored to maintain a correct sequence.

The finest art revolves around keeping track of how soon or late certain cards may be needed; how deep and with what cards they may be safely covered; whether a card should be played on a foundation or held back to develop another foundation.

BETSY ROSS
(Four Kings, Musical Patience, Quadruple, Alliance)
Time required: 5 minutes
Chance of winning: 1 in 8 games

Layout Put in a row any ace, two, three and four. In a second row below put any two, four, six and eight. The lower row comprises the foundations, which are to be built up as follows, regardless of suit:

2, 3, 4, 5, 6, 7, 8, 9, 10, J, Q, K
4, 6, 8, 10, Q, A, 3, 5, 7, 9, J, K
6, 9, Q, 2, 5, 8, J, A, 4, 7, 10, K
8, Q, 3, 7, J, 2, 6, 10, A, 5, 9, K

The function of the top row is merely to remind you of the arithmetical differences by which the foundations are to be built up.

Play Turn up cards from the stock one at a time, putting each either on a foundation or on a single wastepile. The top of this wastepile is always available.

Redeals Two redeals are allowed.

Betsy Ross layout after one play The ♥10 is on top of the wastepile.

Tips Spread the wastepile to keep track of all cards. The most vital point is to avoid reversed sequences in the stock. For example, if three cards turn up in the order of Q-K-J (regardless of whether they are separated by intervening cards), this is a reversed sequence as regards the first foundation. An earlier jack will have to be reversed to take off the Q-K, or these cards will have to go on other foundations if the jack below them is earmarked for the first foundation. The ideal is to select for play on the first redeal only those cards, the removal of which will leave all remaining cards arranged in correct sequence for the foundations on which they are to be played.

KING'S AUDIENCE
(Queen's Audience)
Time required: 4 minutes
Chance of winning: 3 out of 4 games

Layout Deal 16 cards so as to enclose a rectangular space, the 'audience chamber'. The surrounding cards are the 'antechamber'.

Foundations Whenever a jack and ace of the same suit are available at the same time, move them into the audience chamber, the jack on top. The aces are in effect discarded. The jacks are foundations. Build them down in suit to twos.

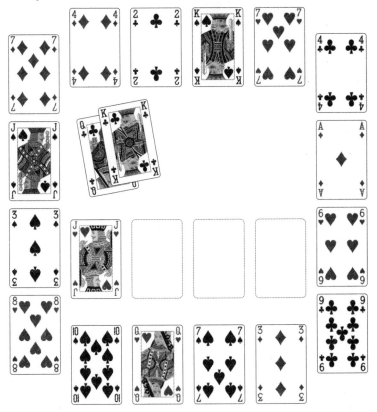

King's Audience after several plays The ♥A is under the ♥J. The ♣Q and ♣K have been discarded. The ♠J may not be played to the foundation row (shown by broken lines) until the ♠A becomes available.

Play Turn up cards from the stock one at a time, putting unplayable cards in a single wastepile. The top of the wastepile is always available. All cards in the antechamber are available for play on foundations. Fill spaces from the wastepile, or, if there is no wastepile, from the stock. Whenever a king and queen of the same suit are both available, discard both. There is no redeal.

CARPET
Time required: 4 minutes
Chance of winning: 3 out of 4 games

Layout Remove the four aces from the pack and put them in two columns, wide apart. Build these foundations up in suit to kings. Between the columns, deal four rows of five cards each, forming a reserve called the 'carpet'. The layout is as follows:

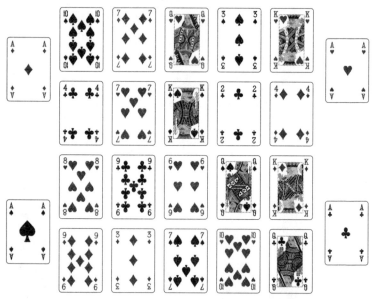

Play Turn up cards from the stock one at a time, putting unplayable cards face up in one wastepile. The top of this pile is always available. All cards of the reserve are available. Fill spaces from the wastepile, or, if there is none, from the stock. There is no redeal.

DUCHESS
(Glenwood)
Time required: 10 minutes
Chance of winning: 1 in 10 games

Layout Deal a reserve of 12 cards, four fans of three cards each. Below the reserve deal four cards in a row for the tableau. Leave room between reserve and tableau for the foundations.

Duchess layout If the ♥5 is selected as a foundation, it is moved to that row (shown by the broken lines) and the ♦5 beside it.

Foundations Select the top card of any one of the reserve fans for the first foundation, and move it below the reserve. Put the other cards of the same rank, as they become available, in a row with the first. Build the foundations up in suit until each pile contains 13 cards; the ranking of cards is continuous, ace above king and below the two.

Tableau building On the tableau, build down in alternate colours. A whole pile must be moved as a unit, when the bottom card of the pile is correct in colour and sequence for building on the top card of another pile. Fill tableau spaces from available reserve cards; and, after the reserve is exhausted, from the wastepile.

83

Play The top cards of the reserve fans are available for building on foundations and tableau, and for filling tableau spaces.

Turn up cards from the stock one at a time, playing them on foundations or tableau. Put unplayable cards in a single wastepile. The top of this pile is always available.

Redeal One redeal is allowed.

FORTUNE'S FAVOUR
Time required: 5 minutes
Chance of winning: 9 out of 10 games

Foundations Remove the four aces from the pack and put them in a row. Build them up in suit to kings.

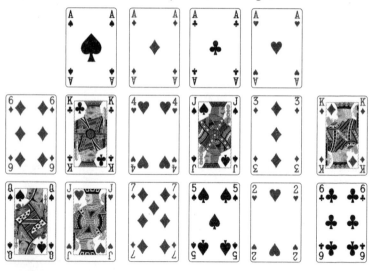

Tableau Deal two rows of six cards each. On this tableau build down in suit. One card at a time may be moved from the top of a pile to another tableau pile or a foundation. Fill spaces in the tableau from the wastepile, or, if there is none, from the stock.

Play Turn up cards from the stock one at a time, playing them on foundations or tableau. Put unplayable cards in a single wastepile. The top of this pile is always available.

GATE

Time required: 8 minutes
Chance of winning: 1 in 10 games

Layout Deal two columns of five cards each, forming the 'posts' (reserve). Between them deal two rows of four cards each, forming the 'rails' (tableau).

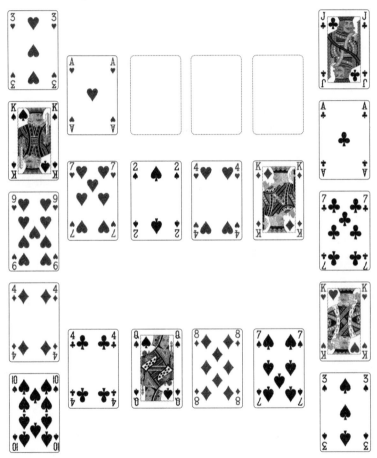

Gate layout After the ♥A has been moved to the foundation row.

Foundations Move the four aces, as they become available, into a row above the 'rails'. Build these foundations up in suit to kings.

Play All cards in the rails, and bottom cards of posts, are available for play on foundations or tableau. On the rails, build downwards in alternate colour. Either the top card or pile as a whole may be lifted up from a rail pile building on another. Fill spaces in the rails from the posts, and, after the posts are exhausted, from the wastepile. Do not fill spaces in the posts. Turn up cards from the stock one at a time, playing them on foundations or rails. Put unplayable cards in a single wastepile. The top of this pile is always available.

TENS
(Take Ten)
Time required: 2 minutes
Chance of winning: 1 in 8 games

Deal 13 cards, in two rows of five and one row of three. Discard pairs of cards that total ten. Discard kings, queens, jacks and tens only in quartets of the same rank. Fill spaces from the stock. The game is won if you can run through the stock without reaching an impasse.

FOURTEEN OUT
(Fourteen Puzzle, Take Fourteen)
Time required: 5 minutes
Chance of winning: 2 out of 3 games

Layout Lay the whole pack in 12 piles, face up. Put five cards in each of the first four piles, four cards in each of the rest. Spread the piles towards yourself so that all cards are in sight.

Play The object of play is to discard the whole layout in pairs of cards that total 14; king being 13, queen 12 and jack 11. Only the top card of each pile is available.

Tips If the two cards totalling 14 lie in one pile, the upper card must be removed as soon as possible, in preference to other available cards of its rank. Take note of all such combinations in the layout, and plan how to break them up, before making any play. Also look for 'criss-crosses' between piles. Suppose, for example, that one pile contains eight and five (reading downwards) and another nine and six. It would be fatal to leave these combinations untouched, while discarding the rest of the fives and sixes.

GOLF

Time required: 4 minutes
Chance of winning: 1 in 20 games

Layout Deal five rows of seven cards each, overlapping the cards to form seven piles spread downward. Deal one additional card to start the wastepile.

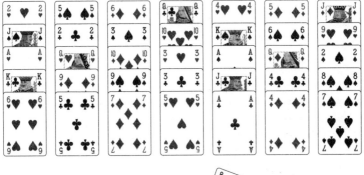

Golf layout The following series of cards can be played off on the wastepile, of which the first card is the ♣8: ♠7, ♠8, ♦7, ♥6, ♥5, ♦4; here there are several choices of continuation, but the best is to clear off an ace, thus: ♣3, ♣4, ♥3, ♠2, ♣A. An alternative line would be: ♣8, ♦7, ♥6, ♠7, ♠8, ♠9, ♦10. This takes off fewer cards; it leaves the remaining available cards well-connected, but so does the first line, which is therefore preferable.

Play Only the top card of each pile is available. The object is to clear away the whole tableau by building the cards upon the wastepile. Build in sequence, up or down, regardless of suit. The option of direction exists on every play; for example, having put a six on a five, you are not bound to continue up, but may go down with another five. The ranking is not, however, 'around the corner'. Only a two may be built on an ace, and a king stops the sequence – a queen may not be built on it.

Each time you find no available cards to build, turn up another card from the stock and lay it on the wastepile.

You win the game if you clear off the tableau; failing that, your object is to leave as few cards in it as possible.

Tips Plan the entire sequence before moving any card from the tableau. With choice between available cards of the same rank, note which of the cards to be uncovered would allow the sequence to be prolonged. With choice between whole sequences, the natural preference is for the longest sequence, but other considerations may supervene, especially at an early stage of the game. It is important, when feasible, to leave available for the next turn a group of cards in sequence rather than unconnected. For example, with a choice of what to uncover in the last play of a sequence, uncover a seven if an eight and a six are exposed elsewhere, rather than an unconnected two, etc.

The most dangerous cards are, of course, kings. So long as any real prospect of winning remains, reserve queens to take off kings.

TOURNAMENT GOLF

This is a method of competitive scoring between two players, each playing nine Golf games with his own pack. A player's score for each game is the number of cards left in the tableau. The scores are compared, game by game, and the lower score for each game earns one point for the 'hole'. A hole may be made in a minus number of strokes – if the player clears off the tableau with cards still left in his stock, he subtracts from his score the number of such cards. The better 'medal' score – total of 'strokes' for the nine holes – earns three points.

Playing solo you may consider that in a round of nine holes you beat 'par' if your medal score is less than 36.

CAPTIVE QUEENS
(Quadrille)
Time required: 4 minutes
Chance of winning: 1 in 2 games

Play Turn up cards from the stock one at a time, putting unplayable cards in a single wastepile. The top of this pile is always available.

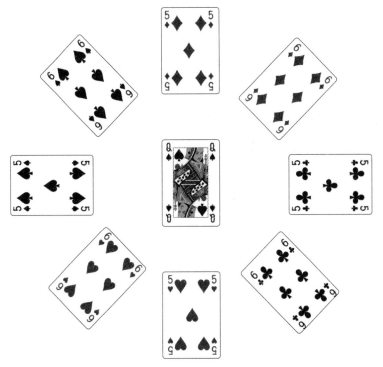

Captive Queens layout Showing traditional position of foundations (fives and sixes) and discarded queens. It is simpler to put the foundations in two rows.

Foundations Put the fives and sixes, as they become available, in a circle. Build the sixes up in suit to jacks; build the fives down in suit to aces, then kings. The queens are thus dead cards. As they turn up discard them in a pile inside the circle of foundations.

Redeals Two redeals are allowed.

MONTE CARLO
(Weddings, Double and Quits)
Time required: 10 minutes
Chance of winning: 1 in 8 games

Layout Deal five rows of five cards each.

Play Discard cards in pairs of the same rank, provided that the two cards of the pair are adjacent in a row, a column or a diagonal. The removal of a card does not make the two cards beside it 'adjacent'.

After removing all possible pairs, consolidate the tableau. That is, back up the remaining cards so as to make the rows solid as far as the cards go, from top down. Keep the cards in the same order as they were dealt, reading from left to right and from top row down. That is, push the cards in the highest incomplete row leftwards, then fill out the row with cards taken one by one from the left end of the row below. After doing this, deal additional cards from the stock so as to fill it out to 25 cards, and resume play. After the stock is exhausted, consolidate the tableau each time all possible plays have been made.

To win the game, you must get the entire pack paired up in the discard.

Tips If a card can be paired with either of two others, pick the pair that will give more additional plays after consolidation. In the diagram, pair the ♥7 with the ♣7, not the ♠7, so as to bring the red twos together.

BLOCK TEN
Time required: 1 minute
Chance of winning: 1 in 10 games

Deal nine cards, in three rows of three each. Deal cards from the stock to cover each pair of cards that total ten, and each pair of face cards (kings, queens, jacks) of the same rank. Ignore suits. A ten blocks further play on the pile it covers.

The game is won if you succeed in dealing the entire pack upon the layout.

Monte Carlo layout Either ♣7 and ♥7, or ♥7 and ♠7 may be discarded; if the ♣7, the ♦J will be moved to the extreme right of the top row, etc.

DOUBLE OR QUITS
Time required: 5 minutes
Chance of winning: 1 in 3 games

Layout Deal two columns of three cards each, then a card between the columns at the top. These seven cards are the reserve. Deal one card between the columns at the bottom; this is the one and only foundation.

If any kings turn up in the layout, remove them and put them on the bottom of the stock. Deal additional cards to replace them.

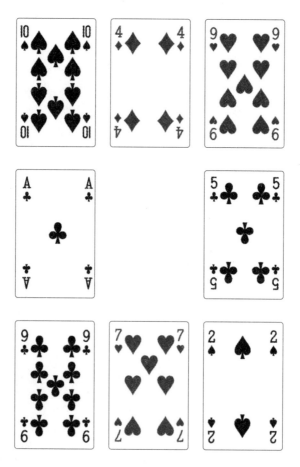

Double or Quits layout The ♥7 is the foundation, the others the reserve.

Play The object of play is to build the entire pack other than kings on the one foundation, in the following continuous sequence: A, 2, 4, 8, 3, 6, Q, J, 9, 5, 10, 7, A, 2, etc.

(This is a doubling sequence, with 13 subtracted each time the result exceeds 12.)

Suits are ignored in building. Kings are dead cards; a king once placed in the reserve (after adjustment of the layout) must stay there.

Turn up cards from the stock one by one, putting unplayable cards face up in one wastepile.

All seven cards of the reserve are available for play on the foundation. Fill a space in the reserve from the top of the wastepile, or, if there is none, from the stock. The top of the wastepile is also available for play on foundations.

Redeals Two redeals are allowed.

NESTOR
(Matrimony)
Time required: 4 minutes
Chance of winning: 1 in 10 games

Layout Deal six rows of eight cards each, overlapping the cards to form eight piles spread downwards, and leaving a stock of only four cards. Do not put two cards of the same rank in the same pile. If, during the deal, a card turns up that duplicates a card already in that pile, place the duplicate on the bottom of the pack and deal the next card instead.

Play The top card of each pile is available. Discard available cards in pairs of the same rank, regardless of suits. Each time you reach a block, turn up the top card of the stock and use it if you can, by discarding it with any available card of the same rank. The game is won if you get the whole pack paired up in the discard. (Evidently the game is lost if you turn a stock card and cannot use it, for by rule it must be discarded. An alternative rule is to turn all four stock cards face up as a reserve, each being available at any time.)

ACES UP
(Firing Squad)
Time required: 2 minutes
Chance of winning: 1 in 10 games

Play Aces are high, ranking above kings. Deal a row of four cards. Discard any card that is lower than another card of the same suit. Deal another row of four cards on the (remainder of the) first batch. Play as before. Continue in the same way, dealing the entire pack four at a time on the same four piles. Discard all lower available cards whenever a higher card of the same suit is at the top of another pile. Fill any space, if possible, prior to the next deal, with a card taken from the top of another pile; this may make possible one or more additional plays before you deal again. Aces obviously may be moved only into spaces. The game is won if only the four aces remain at the end, the rest of the pack having been discarded.

Aces Up after several rows have been dealt Discard the ♥8 (lower than ♥K) and ♣8 (lower than ♣K), then ♥Q and ♣9; move ♣K and ♦9 into the spaces, discard ♥4 and ♣6; move ♥K into the space and deal four more cards.

Tips Use spaces to uncover buried high cards. Do not move aces into spaces automatically – some other snarl may at the time call more urgently for untangling. But whenever an ace covers another card, leave some other pile that *might* be cleared away by a lucky fall of the cards. Often towards the end it can be seen that no fall of the cards can win. Don't be stubborn – pick up the cards and start another game.

BRISTOL
Time required: 5 minutes
Chance of winning: 1 in 3 games

Layout Deal eight fans of three cards each, forming the tableau. If any kings show, move each to the bottom of its fan. Below the tableau, deal a row of three cards, starting the reserve.

Foundations Move the aces, as they become available, to a row above the tableau. Build them up to kings, regardless of suit.

Play Top cards of tableau fans and reserve piles are available to be built on foundations and tableau. On the tableau, build down regardless of suit. One card at a time may be lifted off a fan to be built on the top card of another or on a foundation.

Deal the stock three cards at a time, one on each reserve pile, pausing between deals to play up what you can. Do not fill a space in the reserve except by the next deal. A space in the tableau, by removal of an entire fan, is never filled.

There is no redeal.

Tips The main problem is to untangle reversed sequences in the tableau – any higher card above a lower. Sometimes tableau-building alone will do the trick, but usually you also have to build up one or two foundations in a hurry to remove a blocking high card. Don't overlook that reversed sequences are just as fatal in the reserve as in the tableau. Save everything you can from being buried in the reserve, especially when some kings are yet to come.

EIGHT OFF

Time required: 15 minutes
Chance of winning: 1 in 2 games

Layout Deal eight piles of six cards each, spread downwards so that all cards are visible. The usual method of dealing is by rows. These 48 cards are the tableau. Spread the four remaining cards of the pack separately below the tableau, starting the reserve.

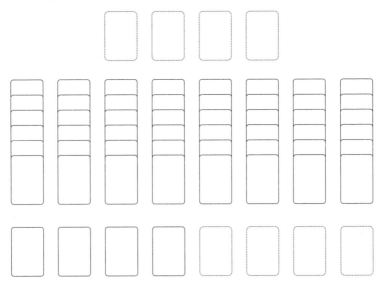

Foundations Move the aces, as they become available, to a row above the tableau. Build them up in suit to kings.

Play Top cards of the tableau piles, and all cards of the reserve, are available to be played on foundations, built on the tableau, or moved to the reserve. On top cards of tableau piles, build down in suit. Only one card at a time may be lifted from a tableau pile to be moved elsewhere.

Any available tableau card may be moved to the reserve, with the proviso that the reserve may never exceed eight cards. In effect, the reserve cards are held out of play, pending the making of a place for them on foundations or in builds on the tableau.

A space in the tableau, made by removing an entire pile, may be filled only by an available king.

Tips Don't overlook that a tableau space has not the same utility as an opening in the reserve. The latter can be used to consolidate builds, e.g., if the ♣7 lies on the ♣8, both can be moved upon the ♣9 by moving the ♣7 momentarily to the reserve. But a tableau space cannot be so used, since it may be filled only by a king. Therefore, do not hurry to make a tableau space merely to absorb a king, at the cost of filling up the reserve. Aim rather to release aces and foundation builders while keeping enough reserve spaces to continue manipulation. Be wary of building too many cards above a lower card of the same suit.

FISSION
Time required: 8 minutes
Chance of winning: 9 out of 10 games

Layout Deal seven piles of seven cards each, spread downwards so that all cards are visible. The usual method of dealing is by columns. These 49 cards are the reserve. Put the last three cards of the pack in a column at the extreme right, forming the tableau.

Play At the outset, only the top cards of the seven reserve piles are available. After playing off the top card, break the column in the middle by pulling the nearest three cards towards you, so as to form two piles of three; the top of each of these piles is available. When a card is played off a pile of three, the remaining two cards are separated and each becomes a foundation.

The tableau may contain four piles; as originally dealt, it therefore includes one space. A space may be filled at any time by an available card from the reserve. On the tableau cards, available cards from the reserve may be built in suit, regardless of rank. Tableau cards may be moved only to be built on foundations, one card at a time being available at the top of a pile.

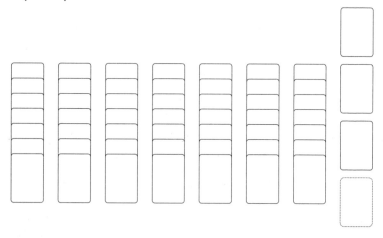

Foundations The 'fission' of each reserve column produces four foundation cards. Build all foundations up in suit and sequence, with the sequence of rank continuous (the ace ranking above the king as well as below the two). Available for foundation building are the top cards of reserve and tableau piles. Foundations of the same suit should be consolidated, when they meet, to save room. The game is won if all four suits are gathered together in sequence.

Tips The paramount consideration is to avoid impasses in tableau building. Obviously if an eight is placed on a seven, the game can never be won. The eight might safely be laid on the six, however, if the seven is in such a position in the reserve that it will eventually become a foundation. Take note that the cards destined to become foundations in each column are, from top (bottom of the pile) down: first, second, fourth and fifth. Before moving any card from reserve to tableau, trace backward in the suit to locate the foundation that will have to be built up eventually to take it off the tableau. For example, if the ♦2 is in question, find the ♦A, ♦K, ♦Q, etc., so as to note the first of the series that lies in 'foundation position' in its column. Suppose that the ♦Q is the first. Then, to lay the ♦2 on the ♦A or ♦K in the tableau would be fatal, for both of these cards are essential to remove the ♦2.

If the original tableau cards chance to be of different suits, you should usually fill the space by a card of the fourth suit. If two or more of the three dealt are of the same suit, aim first of all to move one or two of them onto foundations, so as to make way for all four suits in the tableau. If, for example, none of the four tableau piles is in hearts, all hearts are for the moment immovable. But sometimes you can make inroads on a blocking suit, without a tableau space available, by uncovering some foundations of that suit.

STRATEGY
Time required: 5 minutes
Chance of winning: 1 in 5 games

Play Deal the entire pack, one card at a time. Put the aces, as they turn up, in a foundation row. Put the other 48 cards in eight wastepiles, placing each card on any pile you wish.

After the deal, the top of each pile is available. Build up the aces in suit and sequence to kings. The game is won if you succeed in placing the cards so that at the end they will all play off onto the foundations.

Tips The ideal would be to build descending sequences in suit. But many higher cards are bound to turn up before lower cards of the same suit. The solution is to build partial- and skip-sequences, scattering each suit among the wastepiles in such a way as to keep a specific place reserved for every other card of the same suit yet to come. Obviously, you are blocked if you ever lay a card on a pile containing a lower card of the same suit. Similarly, you can block yourself by making criss-crosses between suits. The easiest way to avoid criss-crosses is to build generally down, whatever the suits, and examine the specific situation whenever you must put any higher card on a lower one.

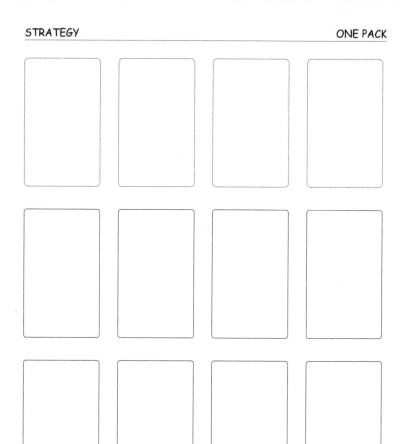

One pile must be reserved at the outset for kings, but once a king is down, the queen of the same suit can be put on it. With almost the same urgency, a pile must be reserved for queens at the outset, and perhaps a third for jacks – at all events, you must be wary of starting a pile with any card lower than a ten, until forced. As the play progresses, note the specific high cards yet to come and keep some piles available to absorb each (by keeping lower cards of the same suit out of the pile).

POKER SOLITAIRE
(Poker Squares)

Turn up 25 cards from the stock, one by one, and place each to the best advantage in a tableau of five rows of five cards each. The object is to make as high a total score as possible, in the ten Poker hands formed by the five rows and five columns. Two methods of scoring are prevalent, as follows:

HAND	BRITISH	AMERICAN
Royal Flush	30	100
Straight Flush	30	75
Four of a kind	16	50
Full house	10	25
Flush	5	20
Straight	12	15
Three of a kind	6	10
Two pairs	3	5
One pair	1	2

The American system is based on the relative likelihood of the hands in regular Poker. The British system is based on the relative difficulty of forming the hands in Poker Solitaire.

You may consider that you have 'won the game' if you total 200 (American) or 70 (British).

CRIBBAGE SOLITAIRE I

Deal six cards face down for your hand, and two face down for the crib. Look at your hand, and lay away two cards to the crib. Turn up the next card of the stock for the starter. Score your hand, then turn up and score your crib.

Put the starter on the bottom of the pack; discard the other eight cards. Deal again and score in the same way. Continue dealing and discarding until only four cards remain in the pack. Turn these up and score them as a hand without a starter.

The object is to make the highest possible total score. By tradition, you are considered to 'win the game' if you reach 120.

CRIBBAGE SOLITAIRE II
(Cribbage Squares)

Turn up 16 cards from the pack, one by one, placing each to best advantage in a tableau of four rows of four cards each. But each card must be put adjacent – horizontally, vertically or diagonally – to a card already in the tableau.

Turn the 17th card for a starter. Score each row and column of the tableau as a Cribbage hand, together with the starter.

The object is to make the highest possible total score. You may consider that you have 'won the game' if you reach 61.

CRIBBAGE SOLITAIRE III
(Bill Beers)

Deal cards in a row, one at a time (not overlapped), and look for the following combinations in each two or three adjacent cards:

COMBINATION	SCORE
One pair	2
Three of a kind	6
Three of the same suit	3
Three in sequence	3
Three in suit and sequence	6
Two or three that total 15	2

As in Cribbage, ace scores 1, each K, Q, J and 10 scores ten. A sequence is valid even if the cards do not lie in sequential order, e.g., 9-7-8 is a scoring combination, as well as 9-8-7.

After scoring any combination, move any one of the cards involved upon any other. Try if possible to make additional scoring combinations by this move. For example, with 9-7-5-6, score the sequence, then move the 6 upon the 7 and score the 15, that is, 9-6.

Each combination must be scored and consolidated at once, before another card is turned from the pack, except that, when a pair shows, a third card may be dealt to see if it becomes a triplet.

The object is to make the highest possible score on running through the entire pack. You may consider that you have 'won the game' if you reach 61.

DOUBLE JUMP
Time required: 5 minutes
Chance of winning: 1 in 20 games

Deal cards in one row from left to right. Whenever two cards, separated from each other by two others, are alike in suit or rank, move the one at the left upon the one at the right. To save room, move the cards leftwards after every jump (which makes a gap in the row), being careful not to change the order of the cards. One jump may make other jumps possible. You win the game if you reduce the row to three piles after the last card is dealt.

SOLITAIRES PLAYED WITH TWO PACKS

SPIDER
Time required: 20 minutes
Chance of winning: 1 in 3 games

Layout Deal 54 cards in ten piles, six cards in each of the first four piles and five cards in each of the rest. The traditional method of dealing is by rows. The top card of each pile should be face up, the rest face down.

Building The ten piles serve as both tableau and foundations. The top card of each pile is always available. Available cards may be built down, regardless of suit, ending at ace. (A king may not be built on an ace; it can be moved only to a space.)

Any or all of the cards on top of a pile, while they are in the same suit as well as in correct (downwards) sequence, may be lifted as a unit to be built elsewhere.

On clearing away all cards above a face-down card, turn it up; it then becomes available. A space made by clearing away an entire pile may be filled by any available card or build.

Discard The object of play is to assemble 13 cards of a suit, in correct sequence. Whenever a suit is so assembled on top of a pile, you may lift it off and discard it. The game is won if you discard the whole pack in eight batches. It is not compulsory to discard a suit when able.

Play Whenever play comes to a standstill, deal another row of ten cards, one upon each pile of the tableau. All spaces must be filled prior to such a deal.

Tips Prefer 'naturals' – builds in suit – where choice offers. Coming before this policy, however, is the rule: make first the builds that you can unmake. For example, if the layout shows two sixes and a five, move the five on a six first, ahead of even a natural build, since the five can be moved later if necessary.

Among builds that are not naturals, start with those of highest rank.

Try to make a space as early as possible. Sometimes this will mean that, having depleted one pile, your prospects are better to continue removing cards from that pile than making natural builds, where choice offers. Use spaces to reshuffle sequences into 'naturals' so far as possible, before finally filling them.

SLY FOX

Time required: 15 minutes
Chance of winning: 5 out of 6 games

Foundations Remove one ace and one king of each suit from the pack. Put them in two columns, at the extreme left and right. Build the aces up in suits to kings, and the kings down in suits to aces.

Sly Fox layout The outlined cards represent the reserve.

Reserve Between the foundation columns deal a reserve of 20 cards, four rows of five each. All these cards are available for play on foundations. If any (of the original 20) is played up, fill the space immediately from the stock.

Play After play comes to a standstill (and with all spaces filled), turn up additional cards, one at a time, from the stock. Play up what you can (and want to) on foundations. Put each unplayable card on any reserve pile you wish. Continue dealing until you have added 20 cards to the reserve (not including cards played on foundations). Only after such addition may you resume playing cards from the reserve to the foundations. Only the top cards of reserve piles are available.

Continue in the same way, adding 20 cards at a time to the reserve before again moving cards out of the reserve. The final deal may, of course, comprise less than 20 cards. Except as to the original deal, spaces in the reserve are not filled at once; but they may be utilised in placing the next batch of 20 cards from the stock. There is no redeal, and no reversal on the foundations (by playing from one foundation pile to another).

Tips If you lose this game, it will probably be by your own error.

The natural policy is to build the reserve piles in suit and sequence. But do not push this to the point of blocking yourself. For example, if you put a ♠5 above a ♠6, don't put the other ♠5 over the other ♠6. Two builds of duplicate cards must be made in opposite directions.

Some scattering of the cards of a suit is inevitable, if only to avoid such blocks. Beware of a 'criss-cross' between suits. For example, if you put an ♦A over a ♣2, don't put an ♣A over a ♦2. This block can be broken in theory – by building one of the kings down to two, while putting nothing on the ace of the same suit – but this theoretical resolution is rarely feasible. Similar criss-crosses among middling cards are less hazardous, but be sure to use their duplicates to untangle them.

One pile of the reserve may well be earmarked for the four aces and kings wanted last on the foundations. By the same token, these end cards can be heaped on a queen or a two, provided only that the king or ace of the same suit is put in a space.

FROG
(Toad)
Time required: 15 minutes
Chance of winning: 1 in 5 games

Reserve Deal a pile of 13 cards, holding out any aces that turn up. Square up the pile and put it at the left.

Foundations Put aces in a row at the right of the reserve. If no ace has turned up in dealing the reserve, remove one ace from the stock. Put all remaining aces, as they become available, in a row with the first. Build them up to kings, regardless of suits.

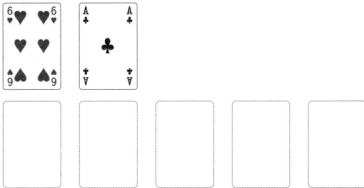

Frog layout The ♥6 tops the reserve pile, the ♣A has been set out as first foundation; the broken lines indicate the positions of the wastepiles.

Play Turn up cards from the stock one at a time, putting unplayable cards on any of five wastepiles. You may put each card where you wish, provided that you make no more than five piles. The top card of each wastepile and the top card of the reserve, are always available for play on foundations. There is no redeal.

Tips You had better reserve one wastepile for kings and queens. On other piles, of course, build generally downwards, in sequence when able. But of course you will frequently be forced to put a high card on a lower. Then be careful not to mass cards of like rank, subsequently turned, so as to create a block. To imagine an extreme example, suppose that you have covered a six with a jack. Then, to add all remaining unplayed sevens to the same pile would be fatal. Of course, it would be bad on principle to mass cards of the same rank in one pile. But the position of all other sixes might be such that to put a single seven on this six–jack pile would be fatal. The ideal is to build two or more piles in complementary segments, so that as soon as a foundation is built up to the necessary height all these segments can be skimmed off, exposing the low cards of the segments below.

SALLY
Time required: 15 minutes
Chance of winning: 1 in 10 games

Follow all the rules of Frog, except: deal only 12 cards to the reserve. Do not take out any aces to start the foundation row; all aces must be made available during the course of play.

COLORADO
Time required: 15 minutes
Chance of winning: 1 in 10 games

Layout Deal a tableau of 20 cards, in two rows of ten each.

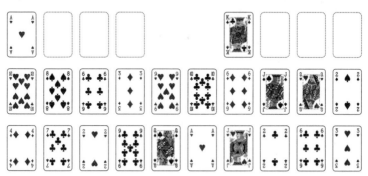

Colorado layout The ♥A and ♣K have been set out as foundations; the other ♥A (in the bottom row) may not be used as a foundation.

Foundations As they become available, move one ace and one king of each suit into a row above the tableau. Build the aces up in suit to kings, and the kings down in suit to aces.

Play Turn up cards from the stock one at a time, putting each on a foundation or on the tableau. You may lay the card on any tableau pile without regard to suits or rank; the tableau in effect comprises 20 wastepiles. Each card must be placed before the next is turned.

The top card of each tableau pile is available for play on foundations; it may be moved for no other purpose. A space in the tableau must be filled at once from the stock. It is not permissible to look at the next card from the stock before deciding whether to make a space. There is no redeal.

CONSTITUTION
Time required: 20 minutes
Chance of winning: 5 out of 6 games

Layout Remove from the pack all aces, kings and queens. Discard the kings and queens. Put the aces in a row for foundations. Below them deal a tableau of 32 cards, in four rows of eight each.

Foundations Build the aces up in suit to jacks.

Tableau Cards may be moved from the tableau to foundations only from the top row. On the cards in the top row you may build down in alternate colours; available for building are the top cards in the top row and all cards of the second row. The top card of a build is available for play on a foundation, but not into a space.

A space in any row must be filled at once by moving up a card from the row below. This can be any card from the lower row, not necessarily the one directly under the space. Each space is thus pushed downwards until it reaches the bottom row, where it must be filled at once from the stock.

Play Note that stock cards get into play only through spaces in the tableau; they may not be played directly to foundations. Therefore, if no more spaces can be made at a time when any of the stock remains undealt, the game is lost.

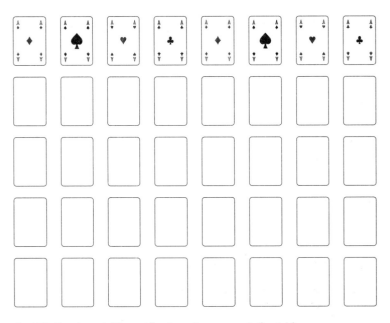

Constitution layout The outlined cards represent the tableau.

Tips If the tableau is notably deficient in twos or other low cards, plan at once to accommodate a larger number of cards in builds. The way to do this is to get a high card, preferably a jack or ten into the top row quickly, and bring up 'feeders' for this pile from below. In any case, be wary of building on middling-low base cards, say fours to sevens, for such builds do not 'pull their weight' in the struggle to make place for new cards.

Generally speaking, move up the lowest card of each row. Certainly, twos, threes and fours must be moved up quickly.

Remember that there are two ways to get a card to a foundation from the second row. One way is to make a space in the first row and move the card up. The other way is to build the card on a first-row pile in passing, as it were. This second way makes a space in the second row but not in the first; it is preferable when the prime consideration is to bring new cards into the tableau (because it is deficient in low cards).

NAPOLEON AT ST HELENA
(Forty Thieves)
Time required: 20 minutes
Chance of winning: 1 in 10 games

Layout Deal a tableau of 40 cards, four rows of ten each, overlapping the cards to form piles spread downwards.

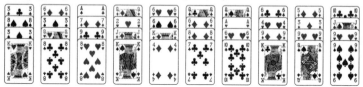

Napoleon at St Helena layout The ♠Q may be built on ♠K, then ♥8 on ♥9, then ♣9 on ♣10, ♣8 on ♣9, etc.

Foundations Move the eight aces, as they become available, to a row above the tableau. Build them up in suits to kings.

Play The top cards of tableau piles are available for play on foundations or on each other. Only one card at a time may be moved. On the tableau, build down in suit. A space made by clearing away an entire column may be filled by any available card from the tableau or from the wastepile.

Turn up cards from the stock one at a time, putting unplayable cards in a single wastepile. The top card of this pile is always available for play on foundations or tableau.

Tips You are entitled to see the next card from the stock before making any decision. Use this privilege.

Drive for a space as soon as possible. This will often involve picking out a pile that has best chance of being cleared away, and refraining from making builds that would usurp the place earmarked for cards in this pile.

LIMITED
Time required: 20 minutes
Chance of winning: 1 in 5 games

Follow all the rules of Napoleon at St Helena, except: deal the tableau in three rows of 12 cards each, to form 12 spread piles. This makes a much better game than Napoleon at St Helena, since fewer cards are out of play.

LUCAS
Time required: 15 minutes
Chance of winning: 1 in 3 games

Follow all the rules of Napoleon at St Helena, except: remove the eight aces and put them in the foundation row. For the tableau, deal three rows of 13 cards each to form 13 spread piles.

MARIA
Time required: 20 minutes
Chance of winning: 1 in 8 games

Follow all the rules of Napoleon at St Helena, except: deal the tableau in four rows of nine cards each, to form nine spread piles; on the tableau, build down in alternate colours.

NUMBER TEN
Time required: 20 minutes
Chance of winning: 1 in 10 games

Follow all the rules of Napoleon at St Helena, except: deal the first two rows of tableau cards face down, the other two face up. On the tops of tableau piles, build down in alternate colours. All cards on top of a pile that are in correct sequence may be lifted as a unit for transfer to another pile.

RANK AND FILE
Time required: 20 minutes
Chance of winning: 1 in 10 games

Follow all the rules of Napoleon at St Helena, except: deal the first three rows of the tableau face down, the last face up. On the tops of tableau piles, build down in alternate colours. All cards on top of a pile that are in correct sequence may be lifted as a unit for transfer to another pile.

INDIAN
Time required: 20 minutes
Chance of winning: 1 in 2 games

Follow all the rules of Napoleon at St Helena, except: deal only 30 cards to the tableau, a row of ten face down, then two rows face up, forming spread piles. In tableau-building, a card may be put on the next-higher card of any suit but its own.

WINDMILL
(Propellor)
Time required: 5 minutes
Chance of winning: 1 in 10 games

Layout Remove any one ace from the pack and place it in the centre of the table, for the first foundation. Deal four 'sails' (reserve) of two cards each around the ace, two in column above, two in column below, two in a row on each side.

Foundations Build the ace up, regardless of suits, until the pile contains 52 cards. Sequence is continuous, ace ranking above king and below two.

Move the first four kings (of any suits) that become available into the spaces between the sails. Build these foundations down, regardless of suits, to aces.

The top card of a king-foundation may be transferred to the ace-foundation, i.e., one card at a time. After such a transfer, the next card put on the ace-foundation must come from elsewhere.

Play The eight cards of the sails are always available for play on foundations. A space in the sails must be filled at once from the wastepile, or, if there is no wastepile, from the stock.

Turn up cards from the stock one at a time, putting unplayable cards in a single wastepile, the top card of which is always available for play on foundations. There is no redeal.

Tips Build up the centre pile at every opportunity. But don't move cards from the sails to the king-foundations until the wastepile shows a card you need to save. The ideal is to have a wide assortment of ranks in the sails and on king-foundations, for feeding of the voracious centre pile. Don't make spaces in such a hurry that you load down the sails with three or four cards of the same rank.

The usual rule is that the foundation kings themselves may not be reversed on to the ace-foundation. Maybe you will want to eliminate this rule – after you discover that winning the game is not so easy as it seems.

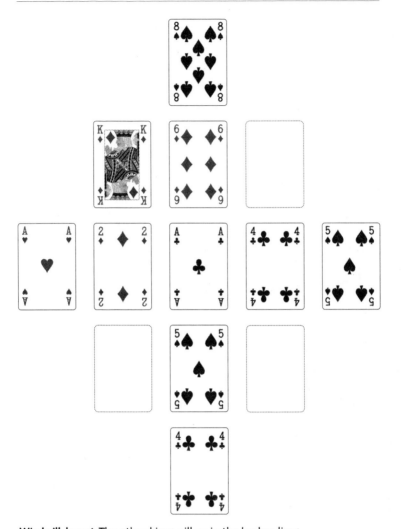

Windmill layout The other kings will go in the broken lines.

MOUNT OLYMPUS
Time required: 15 minutes
Chance of winning: 5 out of 6 games

Foundations Remove all the aces and twos from the pack and put them in two rows. Build these foundations up in suit, by twos, as follows:

A, 3, 5, 7, 9, J, K
2, 4, 6, 8, 10, Q

Tableau Deal a row of nine cards below the foundations. All these cards are available for play on foundations, and for building on each other. Build downwards in suit, by twos. All the cards on top of a tableau pile that are in correct suit and sequence may be lifted as a unit for transfer to another pile. A space in the tableau made by removing an entire pile must be filled from the stock.

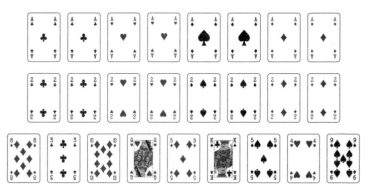

Play Whenever play comes to a standstill, deal another row of nine cards upon the tableau piles. All spaces must be filled before such a deal. Top cards of the piles are always available for building on foundations or tableau.

Tips Spread the piles downwards in column, so as to see all cards. Watch out for reversed sequences (higher card dealt on a lower, whether or not any cards intervene). Plan the building primarily to resolve such reversals.

The game takes its name from the traditional layout – foundations in one curved row, tableau in pyramidal form below. This layout is too wide for the normal-size folding card table, and does not allow for spreading the tableau piles.

GRAND DUCHESS
Time required: 15 minutes
Chance of winning: 1 in 10 games

Foundations As they become available, move one ace and one king of each suit to a foundation row. Build the aces in suit up to kings, and the kings down in suit to aces.

Grand Duchess layout The bottom row is the tableau, the face-down cards the reserve, the ace and king have been set out as foundations.

Play Deal a row of four cards to start the tableau, then two cards face down in a pile to start the reserve.

Play up what you can from the tableau to the foundations. Do not fill spaces except by the next deal.

Continue dealing the whole stock in the same way – four cards to the tableau, one on each pile, and two face down to the reserve. Pause after each deal to play what you can, the top card of each tableau pile being available.

After the stock is exhausted, turn over all cards of the reserve and play what you can on foundations. Continue play from the tableau also, if reserve cards make new plays possible.

Redeals Three redeals are allowed. To form the new stock, pick up the tableau piles in reverse order (each pile on its right-hand neighbour) so that the last-dealt will be at the top of the stock. Then put the unplayed reserve cards on the bottom of the new stock.

In the last redeal, do not give any cards to the reserve: deal the whole stock to the tableau, four cards at a time.

PARISIENNE
Time required: 15 minutes
Chance of winning: 1 in 10 games

Follow all the rules of Grand Duchess, except: Remove one ace and one king of each suit from the pack at the outset and put them in the foundation row.

SALIC LAW
Time required: 15 minutes
Chance of winning: 1 in 3 games

Layout Remove any one king from the pack and put it at the left. Deal cards upon it, overlapping to form a pile spread downwards, until another king turns up. Put the second king at the right of the first, and start dealing a new pile on it. Continue in the same way until the whole pack is laid out in piles, which may be of irregular length, upon the eight kings.

During the deal, hold out all aces and queens. Put the aces in a row above the kings. The queens are dead cards; you may discard them in a pile, or place them in a row above the aces.

Foundations The aces are the foundations. Build them up to jacks, regardless of suits.

Play The top cards of the tableau piles are available for foundation-building – during the deal as well as after it is completed. A bare king, all cards having been played off it, is the equivalent of a space; any available card may be moved upon the king. But spaces may not be utilised until after the deal is completed.

Tips Use the privilege of building on the foundations during the deal to assure that you will be able to make at least one space. Except for this purpose, do not build foundations too high – say beyond four or five.

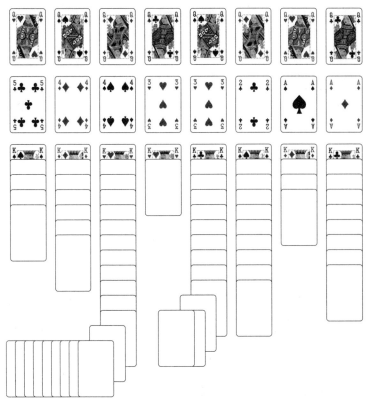

Salic Law layout The foundations, started as aces, have been built up to the levels shown. The outlines represent face-up cards.

TITANIA
Time required: 15 minutes
Chance of winning: 3 out of 4 games

Follow all the rules of Salic Law except: do not discard the queens from the pack. Build the foundations up to queens. After the deal is complete, available cards may be built downwards on the top tableau cards, regardless of suit. Only one card may be moved at a time.

INTRIGUE
Time required: 15 minutes
Chance of winning: 1 in 3 games

Layout Remove any one queen from the pack and put it at the left. Deal cards upon it in a pile of overlapping cards spread downwards until another queen turns up. Put the second queen at the right of the first and start dealing a new pile on it. Continue in the same way until the whole pack is laid out in piles, which may be of irregular length, upon the eight queens.

During the deal, hold out all fives and sixes, and put them in two rows above the queens.

Foundations Build the sixes up to jacks, regardless of suits, and the fives down to aces, then kings, regardless of suits.

Play The top cards of the tableau piles are available for play on foundations, during the deal as well as after it is completed. If all covering cards are removed from a queen, creating a space, any available card may be moved there.

LAGGARD LADY
Time required: 15 minutes
Chance of winning: 1 in 4 games

Follow all the rules of Intrigue, except that fives and sixes may not be moved up faster than queens. For example, if a third six turns up when only two queens are in place, it cannot be put in the foundation row but must be laid on the tableau.

GLENCOE
Time required: 15 minutes
Chance of winning: 1 in 10 games

Follow all the rules of Intrigue, except: each five and six must be placed in column above a queen of their own suit. If there is no appropriate queen at the time a foundation card turns up, it must be dealt upon the tableau.

TOURNAMENT
Time required: 15 minutes
Chance of winning: 1 in 4 games

Layout Deal two columns of four cards each, at left and right. These are the 'kibitzers' (reserve). If no ace or king shows up, shuffle the pack and start again – without opportunity to make an immediate space in the reserve, the game is hopeless.

Between the kibitzers, deal the 'dormitzers' (tableau), four rows of six cards each, overlapping the rows to form four-card piles, spread downward.

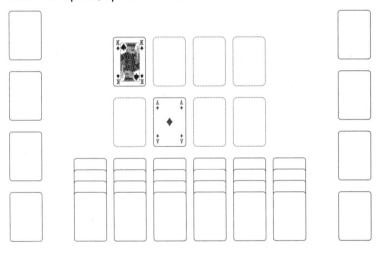

Tournament layout The outlines represent cards dealt face up; the broken lines the positions of foundations as they are set out.

Foundations Move one ace and one king of each suit, as they become available, to rows above the tableau. These foundations are the 'players'. Build the aces up in suit to kings, and the kings down in suit to aces.

Play All cards of the reserve and the top card of each tableau pile are available for play on foundations. A space in the reserve may be filled by any available card from the tableau; you may hold a space open as long as you please. A space in the tableau, made by removing an entire pile, must be filled at once with a pile of four cards from the pack.

Whenever play comes to a standstill, deal four more rows on the tableau, thus adding four overlapping cards to each pile. If less than 24 cards remain in the stock, deal them as far as they will go.

Reversal When the two foundations of a suit meet, the top cards being in sequence, any or all cards of one may be reversed upon the other, including the ace or king at bottom.

Redeals Two redeals are allowed. To form the new stock, pick up the tableau piles (not the reserve) in reverse order, so that the last pile dealt will come to the top of the stock.

Tips Keep at least one space continuously in the reserve, filling it only when this means you will regain a space. In the early play, be wary of putting 'dead' cards in the reserve, i.e., those that are wanted last or late on foundations. When foundations have met, it may be advantageous to hold them intact so that the reversal privilege can be used to dig down to a vital buried card. Generally speaking, if foundations meet during the first redeal, hold them intact until the second redeal, unless there is the possibility of adding several cards to both. Towards the end of the first redeal, try to make many reserve spaces – four or more – rather than to build at the sacrifice of spaces. (But building two foundations to the meeting point is worth some sacrifice.) In the second redeal, try not to let any soon-wanted cards be buried.

NIVERNAISE
(Napoleon's Flank)
Time required: 20 minutes
Chance of winning: 1 in 20 games

Follow the rules of Tournament with these exceptions: deal cards to the tableau in packets, face down, and square them up before turning them over. You may inspect only as many cards at the top of a pile as there are spaces in the reserve. When foundations meet, only one card may be transferred from one to the other.

(The reserve is the 'flanks' and the tableau is the 'line'. Nivernaise is the progenitor of Tournament, but is more tedious and offers less opportunity for skilful planning.)

VIRGINIA REEL

Time required: 20 minutes
Chance of winning: 1 in 4 games

Foundations Remove from the pack a two, three and four, of different suits. Put them in a column at the left. Move all other twos, threes and fours, as the play permits, into rows with these first foundations, all of one rank in one row. You may commence building on a foundation as soon as it is in the row assigned to its rank, but not before. Build up in suit, by threes, as follows:

$$2, \quad 5, \quad 8, \quad J$$
$$3, \quad 6, \quad 9, \quad Q$$
$$4, \quad 7, \quad 10, \quad K$$

Virgina Reel layout The ♠2, ♦3 and ♣4 are the original foundations, and other cards of the same rank will be moved into their respective rows. The outlines represent cards dealt face up.

Tableau Deal 21 cards for a tableau, a row of seven to the right of each of the first foundations. All of these cards are available for play on foundations, but no card may be moved unless the space can be immediately filled by a two, three or four (whichever is called for by the row). Aces are dead cards, and are discarded from the tableau under this same proviso. The card to fill the space comes from the reserve, or may come from another row of the tableau if there is an available reserve card to fill the space in the other row.

If the tableau contains two or three foundations of different ranks, each outside its proper row, they may be exchanged for each other, but only if the exchange will bring each into its proper row. For example, a two in the three-row and a three in the two-row may exchange places. Similarly, a four in the two-row, a three in the four-row and a two in the three-row may be shifted to bring each into its own row.

Play Below the tableau, deal a row of eight cards, forming the reserve. Whenever play comes to a standstill, deal another row of eight cards upon the reserve piles.

Top cards of the reserve piles are always available for play on foundations or (if such top card is a two, three or four) to replace cards moved from the tableau. Do not fill spaces in the reserve except by the ensuing deal of eight cards. Discard aces from the reserve directly after each deal.

Redeals There is no redeal.

Tips The first consideration is to avoid burying foundation cards in the reserve, through inability to make spaces in the tableau. Therefore do not make cyclical shifts in the tableau merely because you can. Such shifts do not make spaces. A foundation in the wrong row may prove of great value, by giving entrance to a foundation card from the reserve. For example, suppose that the three-row is rich in space-making possibilities, while the four-row is not. Then a three in the four-row should be held there until a four is dealt in the reserve.

But a cyclical shift in the tableau may be advisable to save a low card from early burial – a five, six or seven.

Watch for reversals in reserve piles – a higher card over a lower card of the same suit, wanted on the same foundation. Evidently, such a reversal can be resolved only by the play of the upper card on a foundation in preference to its duplicate. For example, if a ♥10 lies over a ♥7 (with or without intervening cards), a block will result if this ♥10 is not played up before the other ♥10. Earmark all cards that *must* be played first of the duplicates; accept all reasonable risk to build up the foundations quickly for this purpose.

There is no point in playing up a face card – jack, queen or king – until the last card is dealt, except to resolve a reversal. Likewise, there is rarely any point in playing up the first eight, nine or ten of its suit to appear, if a jack, queen or king of the suit already lies in the reserve, covering no needed card. It is helpful to take note of non-danger formations and piles, e.g. composed wholly of face cards or containing cards wanted on the same foundation in playable sequence. Concentrate on digging into the incipiently dangerous piles. A major point of judgement is whether to play up the first eight, nine or ten of its suit, when both of the end cards (jack, queen or king of the same suit) are still in the stock.

Despite the great scope for skill in this game, you will often encounter a fatal double block or a 'criss-cross'. Perhaps you will decide to play on in the effort to win 'half a game'; after the last card is dealt, draw out any one buried card, and call the game a half-victory if you can then build up all the foundations.

ROYAL PARADE
(Hussars, Three Up, Financier)
Time required: 15 minutes
Chance of winning: 1 in 30 games

This is the same as Virginia Reel, except that no foundations are put in place at the outset. The tableau comprises 24 cards, three rows of eight each. The urgency of getting foundations into position so far overrides all other considerations as to destroy nearly all opportunity for skill. The chance of winning the game is slight.

CONGRESS
Time required: 10 minutes
Chance of winning: 1 in 30 games

Layout Deal eight cards in two columns of four each, with room between them for two more columns. These cards form the tableau.

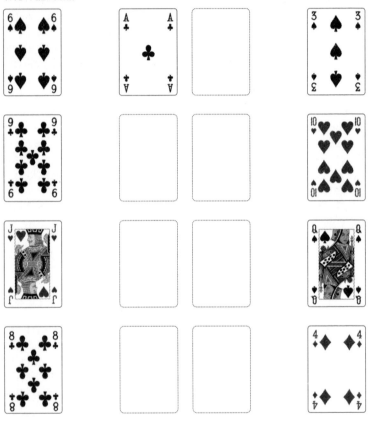

Congress layout The broken lines will be filled by aces.

Foundations Move the eight aces, as they become available, into columns in the centre. Build them up in suits to kings.

Play On the tableau, build together regardless of suit. Only one card at a time may be lifted from the top of a pile, for

128

building on a foundation or on the top of another tableau pile. A space must be filled at once from the wastepile or stock.

Turn up cards from the stock one at a time, putting unplayable cards in a single wastepile, the top card of which is always available. There is no redeal.

Tips Custom allows the player to peek at the next card from the stock before deciding whether to fill a space from stock or wastepile. But the space must be filled before another card is laid on the wastepile. Therefore, do not make spaces by tableau building merely because you can; wait until the wastepile shows a card worth saving. Don't clutter up the tableau with face cards, except when such cards permit space-making builds. Similarly, before moving a card from tableau to foundations, judge whether the card will be more useful kept in the tableau in order to save lower cards from burial in the wastepile.

RED AND BLACK
(Rouge et Noir)
Time required: 10 minutes
Chance of winning: 5 out of 6 games

Foundations Remove the eight aces from the pack and put them in a row. Build them up in alternate colours to kings.

Tableau Below the aces deal a row of eight cards, forming the tableau. These cards may be built down in alternate colours. One card at a time (the top card) may be lifted from a tableau pile for transfer either to a foundation or to the top card of another pile. Spaces in the tableau must be filled at once from the wastepile or, if there is none, from the stock.

Play Turn up cards from the stock one at a time, putting unplayable cards in a single wastepile, the top card of which is always available.

Redeal One redeal is allowed. (An alternative rule to make the game less easy is: no redeal, but tableau piles may be lifted as units in building.)

CORNERSTONES
(Four Corners)
Time required: 20 minutes
Chance of winning: 1 in 2 games

Tableau Deal two columns of six cards each, leaving room between them for two columns of foundations; this begins the tableau. Turn the top and bottom cards of each column sidewise; these four cards are the 'cornerstones'. Continue dealing the whole pack in rotation on the 12 piles, pausing to play up what you can to the foundations, under the rules below.

Foundations As they show up, put one ace and one king of each suit in the centre (see next page). Lay the ace and king of the same suit in the same row, aligned with a row of the tableau (one of the four inner rows, not the cornerstones). Put the aces in one column, the kings in another, and fill these columns in order from top to bottom.

Build the aces up in suit to kings, and the kings down in suit to aces.

Early play During the deal, play up what you can from the stock (not from cards already laid on the tableau). A card that would otherwise fall on a cornerstone may be played on any foundation. However, a card that would fall on any other pile may be played only on a foundation in the row of that pile. The foundation aces and kings may be played from any piles.

Do not skip any tableau pile in dealing. If a pile is deprived of a card because that card was played to a foundation, deal the next card to it.

Later play After the whole stock has been dealt, the top card of every tableau pile is available for play on any foundation, also for building on the top card of another pile. On the tableau, build either up or down, regardless of suit. Sequence of rank is continuous, ace being below the two and above the king. You may reverse the direction of builds on the same pile.

When two foundations of the same suit meet, the top cards being in sequence, any or all cards of one may be reversed upon the other, except the ace or king at bottom.

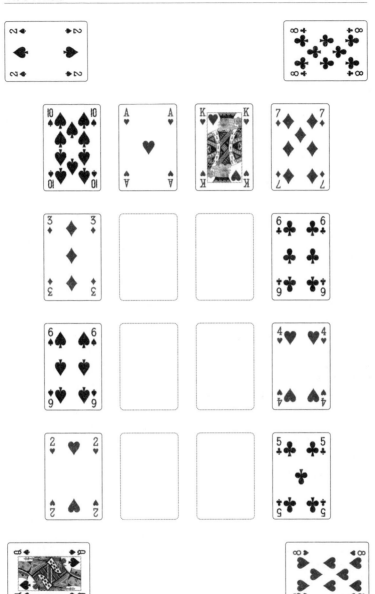

Cornerstones layout As aces and kings of other suits become available, the aces will go in the columns below the ♥A, the kings below the ♥K.

LEONI'S OWN
(Weavers)
Time required: 20 minutes
Chance of winning: 1 in 6 games

Foundations Remove from the pack one ace and one king of each suit and put these foundations in two rows. Build the aces up in suit to kings, and the kings down in suit to aces.

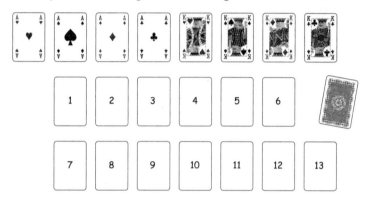

Tableau Deal the rest of the pack in rotation to 13 piles (as far as it goes), forming the tableau. Think of the piles as being numbered from 1 to 13 (or ace to king). When a card turned from the stock would fall on the pile of its own rank (number), put it instead in a 14th pile, face down. The cards so cast out are 'exiles'. Do not skip any tableau pile in dealing; when a card is exiled, deal the next to the pile that would otherwise have received it.

Play After the deal is complete, spread the cards of the 13th or king pile. All the cards of this pile, including cards added later, are available for play on foundations. Also available is the top card of every other pile. Play up what you can.

Whenever play comes to a standstill, turn up the top card of the exile pile. If this card is playable on a foundation, it must be so played. If it is not playable, put it under the pile of its own rank, remove the top card of that pile and put it under the pile of its rank, and so on. Continue shifting cards in this way until a playable card is bared on top of a pile. After putting the card just removed under the proper pile, play up the bared card. Make any additional plays opened up.

When an exile card, or any other reached by shifting, is a king, it halts the shifting. Put the king with the cards from the 13th pile and turn up the next exile. If a stalemate develops on any pile, that deal is ended.

Reversal When two foundations of the same suit meet, with the top cards in sequence, any or all cards of one pile may be reversed on the other, except the ace or king at the bottom.

The rule that an exile or a card bared by shifting must be played if possible does not apply for two foundations at the reversible stage. This is because to do so would rule out the opportunity for making an advantageous move by reversal.

Redeals Two redeals are allowed. To form the new stock, pick up the piles in reverse order (each on its right-hand neighbour) so that the 13th pile will be at the top of the new stock.

INTELLIGENCE
Time required: 30 minutes
Chance of winning: 1 in 6 games

Layout Deal a tableau of 54 cards, in 18 fans of three cards each. When aces turn up in dealing, put them in a foundation row and replace them with other cards.

Foundations Move all aces, as they become available, to a row. Build them up in suit to kings.

Play Top cards of the fans are available to be played on foundations or on each other. In the tableau, build in suit, up or down as you please. You may reverse direction on the same pile. A space made by clearing away an entire fan may be filled by a new fan of three cards from the stock. (This is the only way cards from the stock can be brought into play.)

Redeals Two redeals are allowed. To form the new stock, gather the old stock with the entire tableau and shuffle. As in the original deal, aces (no other cards) may be moved to the foundation row if they turn up in redealing.

HOUSE IN THE WOOD
(Double Fan)
Time required: 20 minutes
Chance of winning: 5 out of 6 games

Layout Deal out the entire pack in a tableau of fans of three cards each, i.e. 34 fans of three and one fan of two.

Foundations Move each ace, as it becomes available, to a foundation row. Build up in suit to kings.

Play Top cards of the fans are available for play on foundations or on each other. On the tableau, build in suit, up or down as you please. You may reverse direction of builds on the same fan. Sequence of rank is not continuous: only a queen may be built on a king, only a two on an ace. Do not fill a space made by clearing away an entire fan. There is no redeal and no reversal on foundations.

Tips Note all fans containing two or more cards of the same suit and plan first of all to dig out these cards. Remember that building up is a temporary expedient, necessary perhaps to reach buried cards, but that all such builds must eventually be reversed into down-builds to be playable on foundations.

HOUSE ON THE HILL
Time required: 20 minutes
Chance of winning: 5 out of 6 games

Follow all the rules of House in the Wood, except: foundation cards are one ace and one king of each suit. Build the aces up in suit to kings and kings down in suit to aces.

Tips Note the bottom cards of all fans; earmark very high or very low cards to be the bases for extensive builds. When foundations meet, before building them further, check that all remaining cards of the suit are in sequences of the right direction to be playable.

THE PLOT
Time required: 10 minutes
Chance of winning: 1 in 2 games

Layout Deal a pile of 13 cards to form the reserve. Since you should see only the top card of this pile, count off the cards face down and square them up before turning them over.

Deal the next card (14th) far to the left; this is the first foundation.

Between the foundation and reserve, deal three rows of four cards each, forming the tableau.

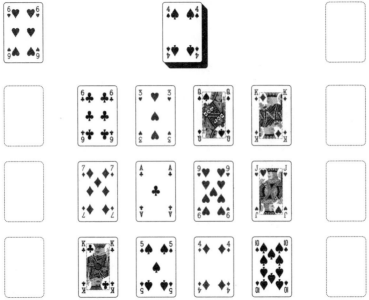

The Plot layout The spaces shown by the broken lines will be filled by sixes.

Foundations As they become available (and subject to the rule below) move the other seven cards of same rank as the first foundation into two columns, one on each side of the tableau. Build them up regardless of suit, until each pile contains 13 cards.

No other foundation may be moved into place until the first foundation has been built to the end. As soon as it is complete, all remaining foundations may be moved up from the tableau, reserve, wastepile and stock.

Play The top card of reserve is available to be played on a foundation.

On the tops of tableau piles, build down regardless of suit. Only one card at a time may be moved from the top of a pile to be played on foundations or tableau. No foundation card may be built, or built upon, in the tableau; such a card turned from the stock before the first foundation is complete must be put on the wastepile.

Until the first foundation is complete, a space in the tableau may be filled only by a foundation card from wastepile or stock. Thereafter, a space may be filled by any card from wastepile or stock (never from tableau or reserve).

Turn up cards from the stock one at a time, playing what you can on tableau and foundations. Put unplayable cards in a single wastepile, the top card of which is available. There is no redeal.

Tips Clearly, you must build up the first foundation as fast as possible. Play from the reserve at every opportunity – it may contain foundation cards or soon-wanted builders.

The rules do not compel filling a space at once. Take advantage of this rule. Keep a space open until a vital card turns up from the stock.

DIPLOMAT
Time required: 15 minutes
Chance of winning: 2 out of 3 games

Layout Deal a tableau in two wings, each wing comprising four rows of four cards each, with the cards overlapping in rows. The usual method of dealing is by columns, alternately to each wing.

Foundations As they become available, move the eight aces into two columns between the wings. Build them up in suit to kings.

Diplomat layout The outlines represent cards dealt face up; the broken lines will be filled by aces.

Play The end card (top of the pile) of each tableau row is available. On the tableau, build down regardless of suit. A space made by clearing away a row may be filled by any available card.

Turn up cards from the stock one at a time, putting unplayable cards in a single wastepile. The top of this pile is always available for play on foundations or tableau. There is no redeal.

TERRACE
(Queen of Italy)
Time required: 15 minutes
Chance of winning: 3 out of 4 games

Layout Deal 11 cards as a row of overlapping cards, to form the reserve. Below, deal a row of three cards. Having inspected the reserve, choose one of these three cards for the first foundation. Move the two rejected cards (if not of the same rank as the chosen card) down to a third row, and deal seven more cards to this row, making nine in all. These nine cards form the tableau.

Terrace layout The overlapped row at the top is the reserve; the ♦7, ♥J and ♣6 were dealt next and the ♣6 was selected as the first foundation.

Foundations As they become available, move all other cards of same rank as the first foundation into the row with it. Build the foundations up in alternate colours until each pile contains 13 cards. The ranking of cards is continuous, ace being above the king and below the two.

Play The reserve cards are available one at a time, from right (top of the pile) to left. They may be played only on foundations.

Tableau cards may be built on foundations and on each other. On the tableau, build down in alternate colours. Only one card at a time may be moved from the top of a tableau pile. A space made by clearing away a whole pile must be filled

138

at once from the wastepile or stock (never from the reserve or tableau).

Turn up cards from the stock one at a time, putting unplayable cards in a single wastepile. The top card of this pile is always available.

Tips In choosing the foundation, keep in mind the following: (1) try to avoid a rank of which several cards are buried in the reserve; (2) try to choose a rank that splits one or more of the reversed sequences in the reserve.

Two cards are in reversed sequence if one card wanted later on the same foundation lies over one wanted earlier (whether or not other cards intervene in the pile). For example, suppose the top card is the ♥8 and the fifth card is the ♣5. If the chosen foundation-rank is four, the red fours must be built up thus: black five, red six, black seven, red eight. Hence the ♥8 and ♣5 lie reversed. However, the selection of any card of an intermediate rank will 'split' the two cards and put them into a normal order, e.g. if the foundation cards are sixes, the eight will be wanted before the five.

Of course, the candidates for foundation may include no card of the desired rank, or, the reserve may contain more reverses than can be split by any one selection. Reverses must sometimes be resolved by careful play. Earmark one foundation to take off the upper card of each reverse; don't build up foundations willy-nilly and leave one blocked by the reserve.

A block can occur by 'criss-cross' among buried cards of the reserve and wastepile. The best insurance against this is to build on a foundation only for the benefit of the reserve card available at the moment. Rarely do you need to depart from this policy – the liberal tableau will give you lots of opportunities to save from the wastepile cards that will be needed later to take off reserve cards.

Don't build on a single tableau card merely because you can. Once it is covered, you cannot turn it into a space except by building off the whole pile on foundations. Try to start the building on the last-wanted ranks, e.g. on sevens, sixes, fives, if the foundations are eights. Save the soon-wanted cards uncovered, so as to make spaces when other soon-wanted cards turn up from the stock. Keep a variety of ranks available.

Once a build has been started, the only reason to refrain from building it at every opportunity is to keep the chance to make a space.

PATIO
Time required: 15 minutes
Chance of winning: 1 in 6 games

Follow the rules of Terrace except as modified: Deal 10 cards to the reserve. Then deal the tableau of nine cards. Deal the next (20th) card for the first foundation.

HERRING BONE
Time required: 12 minutes
Chance of winning: 3 out of 4 games

Foundations As they become available, move the eight jacks into a column. Build them down in suit to aces.

Tableau Deal six cards in two rows of three each. These cards may be built up in suit. An entire pile is lifted as a unit to be built on the top card of another pile. Fill spaces at once from the wastepile or stock (never from the tableau).

Play Turn cards up from the stock one at a time, putting unplayable cards in a single wastepile. The top of this pile is always available for play on foundations or tableau.

Kings and queens are dead cards and may be discarded as opportunity arises. When any jack is in place, one king and one queen of the same suit may be discarded. The custom is to place the discards on either side of the jack, askew and partially under it, so that the column of foundations finally makes a herring-bone pattern.

Redeal One redeal is allowed.

Tips You need a large table and a long reach for this traditional layout. It is simpler to put the jacks in a row, with the discards in one row above.

Herring Bone layout As it will look when foundations are laid out and kings and queens discarded. The herring-bone effect is not essential to the game and the foundation jacks may be set out in a row, the kings and queens being simply discarded.

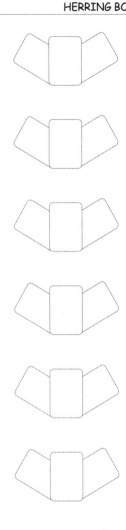

CAPRICIEUSE
Time required: 20 minutes
Chances of winning: 9 out of 10 games

Foundations Remove from the pack one ace and one king of each suit and put them in a row. Build the aces up in suit to kings, and the kings down in suit to aces.

Tableau Deal the rest of the pack into 12 piles, one card at a time to each pile in rotation. (Arrange the piles in any convenient way.)

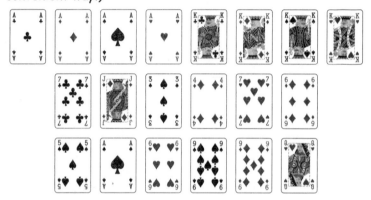

Capricieuse layout The foundation cards (top row) are set out in advance.

Play During the deal, play on the foundations any suitable card turned from the stock. (Do not play from cards already laid on the tableau.) Do not skip a pile in dealing; if a pile is deprived of a card because that card was played on a foundation, play the next card to it.

After the whole stock is dealt, top cards of the tableau piles are available for building on foundations or on each other. On the tableau, build in suit, either down or up. You may reverse direction on the same pile. Sequence of rank is not continuous: only a queen may be built on a king, only a two on an ace.

Redeal Two redeals are allowed. To form the new stock, pick up the 12 tableau piles in reverse order, so that the last-dealt card will be on top.

PRECEDENCE
(Order of Precedence)
Time required: 10 minutes
Chance of winning: 1 in 4 games

Foundations Remove any one king from the pack and put it at the left. As they become available, move any Q, J, 10, 9, 8, 7 and 6 into the same row. These foundations must be moved up in the given order; none may be placed until all the higher ones are in place. All foundations in place may be built on freely. Build down regardless of suits, until each pile contains 13 cards. The ranking of cards is continuous, ace below two and above king.

Play Turn up cards from the stock one at a time, putting unplayable cards in a single wastepile, the top card of which is always available.

Redeals Two redeals are allowed.

ODD AND EVEN
Time required: 10 minutes
Chance of winning: 1 in 10 games

Layout Deal three rows of three cards each, forming the reserve.

Foundations As they become available, move one ace and one two of each suit into a row above the reserve. Build these foundations up in suit, by twos, as follows:

A, 3, 5, 7, 9, J, K, 2, 4, 6, 8, 10, Q
2, 4, 6, 8, 10, Q, A, 3, 5, 7, 9, J, K

Play All cards of the reserve are available for play on foundations. A space in the reserve must be filled at once from the wastepile, or, if there is none, from the stock.

Turn up cards from the stock one at a time, putting unplayable cards in a single wastepile, the top card of which is always available.

Redeal One redeal is allowed.

143

ROYAL COTILLION
Time required: 15 minutes
Chance of winning: 1 in 5 games

Layout Deal 12 cards in three rows of four each, forming the left wing of the tableau. Deal 16 cards in four rows of four, forming the right wing. Leave room between the wings for two additional columns.

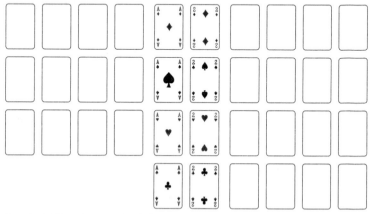

Royal Cotillion layout The left wing is exhausted card by card; the right wing is replenished as each card is moved. The outlines are face-up cards.

Foundations As they become available, move one ace and one two of each suit into the centre columns. Build these foundations up in suit, by twos, as in Odd and Even (page 143).

Play In the left wing, only the bottom card of each column is available, and spaces are never filled. In the right wing, all cards are available, and spaces are filled at once from the wastepile, or, if there is none, from the stock.

Turn cards up from the stock one at a time, putting unplayable cards in one wastepile, the top card of which is always available.

Tips Play from the left wing, this means you can release additional cards. Do not play from the right wing merely because you can; wait to make a space until a card worth saving turns up.

144

GAVOTTE
Time required: 15 minutes
Chance of winning: 1 in 3 games

Follows the rules for Royal Cotillion except for the following modifications: deal 16 cards in both wings, four rows of four. Choose which wing is to be completely available for play; in the other, only bottom cards of columns will be available. Choose any two ranks in sequence for your foundations. (Build up in suit, by twos, until each pile contains 13 cards).

ALHAMBRA
Time required: 10 minutes
Chance of winning: 1 in 10 games

Foundations Remove from the pack one ace and one king of each suit and put them in a row. Build the aces up in suit to kings, and the kings down in suit to aces.

Alhambra layout The foundations aces and kings, in the top row, are set out in advance. The ♦Q may be built on the ♦K. If, for example, the top card of the wastepile is ♠10, either ♠J or else ♠9 and then ♠8 may be built on it.

Reserve Deal a reserve of 32 cards, in eight piles of four cards each. The top card of each pile is available for building on foundations and on the wastepile.

Play Turn up cards from the stock one at a time, putting unplayable cards in a single wastepile. Cards from the reserve may be built on the wastepile, in suit up or down. Sequence of rank is continuous, the ace being below the two and above the king. The top card of the wastepile is available for building on foundations.

Redeals Two redeals are allowed.

145

CRAZY QUILT
(Quilt, Japanese Rug)
Time required: 15 minutes
Chance of winning: 2 out of 3 games

Foundations Remove one ace and one king of each suit from the pack. Put them wherever you find space after dealing the rest of the layout! Build the aces up in suit to kings, and the kings down in suit to aces.

Reserve Deal eight rows of eight cards each, turning alternate cards sideways as shown in the diagram. This is the 'quilt' or 'carpet'. The cards of this reserve become available, for play on foundations or on the wastepile, from the outside in. After the deal, the four cards projecting on each side are available. The removal of any card releases one or two others. The governing rule is: a card is available if it has one of its narrower edges free. For example, in the diagram, removal of the ♣2 releases the ♦7 and ♥3; play of the ♦7 would then release the ♣5.

Play Turn up cards from the stock one at a time, putting unplayable cards in a single wastepile. The top of this pile is always available for play on foundations. Available tableau cards may be built on the wastepile, in suit either up or down. Sequence of rank is continuous, the ace being below the two and above the king.

Redeal One redeal is allowed.

Tips Examine the quilt to see if duplicate cards are both buried remote from the edge. It is usually urgent to dig down to one of these cards as soon as possible. Look for formations that put restrictions on foundation-building. For example, in the diagram, a ♠10 is locked between the ♠4 and ♠6. If you should play the duplicates of these three cards on the ♠A foundation, you would block the game; on the ♠K foundation, the ♠10 must be played before the ♠6 and ♠4. During the first run through the stock, you can do little more than build at every opportunity. But keep track of the

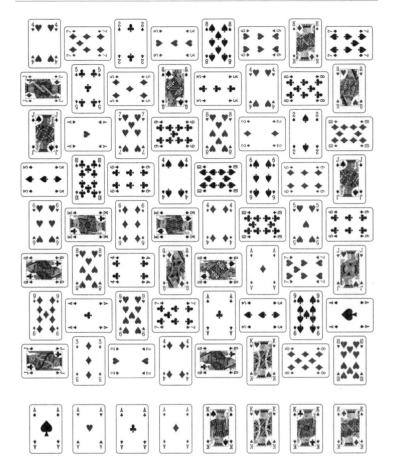

direction of your builds, and play on the foundations in such a way that you avoid blocks.

There is no such thing as an intrinsically 'reversed' sequence among adjacent cards (as there is in some similar games). For example, suppose that you build the ♠5 on the ♠4, and the ♠6 on the ♠5. This trio is capable of being played off on either a ♠3, going up, or a ♠7, going down. In the first case you play off the stock; in the second case, off the wastepile.

Obviously, however, you would be blocked if both of the ♠3 and both of the ♠7 were buried lower in the wastepile on the redeal. You may have to earmark certain cards to go on the up foundation rather than on the down, and vice versa. Such choice exists up to the time that two foundations in the same suit meet, i.e. have been built up so that the top cards are in sequence. Thereafter, each unplayed card can go on only one of the foundations. The idea is to resolve all tangles in each suit before building its foundations to the meeting point.

MATRIMONY

Time required: 15 minutes
Chance of winning: 1 in 30 games

Foundations Remove one ♦Q and one ♦J from the pack. Put them in a foundation row. As they become available, move the following cards into the same row: both ♥J, and the four black tens. Build all foundations in suit as follows: the ♦Q up to ♦J; the jacks down to queens; the tens down to jacks. The ranking of cards is continuous, ace above king and below two.

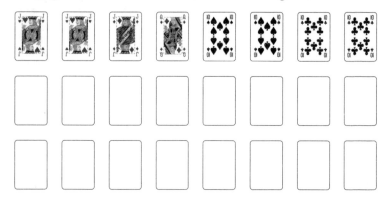

Matrimony layout The top row are foundations; the outlines represent the reserve (dealt face up).

Reserve Below the foundation row, deal a reserve of 16 cards, in two rows of eight each.

Play The top card of each reserve pile is available for play on foundations. Do not fill spaces in the reserve, except by the ensuing deal. Whenever play comes to a standstill, deal 16 more cards, one upon each of the reserve piles, and resume play. The final deal will, of course, comprise only six cards; put them on the first six piles.

After the whole pack has been dealt, and play again comes to a standstill, pick up the 16th pile, turn it over to form a new stock, and deal it on the reserve as far as it goes, commencing at the space left by its removal and continuing with piles 1, 2, 3, etc., in sequence. Continue in the same way: each time play is blocked, deal out the next-lower reserve pile, commencing at its own space. If the game becomes blocked after pile 1 has been dealt out, it is lost.

PARALLELS
Time required: 20 minutes
Chance of winning: 1 in 3 games

Foundations Remove from the pack one ace and one king of each suit. Put them in columns at the extreme left and right. Build the aces up in suit to kings and the kings down in suit to aces.

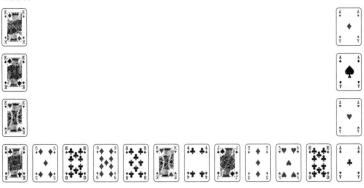

Parallels layout The columns are foundations, set out in advance. There is no play available, so a second row must be dealt to the tableau.

Tableau Between the foundation columns deal a row of ten cards, to start the tableau.

Play All cards of the first tableau row are (always) available for play on foundations. Fill spaces at once from the stock.

With play at a standstill, deal a second row of ten cards below the first (not overlapping). All cards of both rows are available. Fill spaces at once from the stock.

Continue in this way, dealing an additional row of ten cards at the bottom of the tableau whenever play comes to a standstill, observing these rules: only the top and bottom card of each tableau column is available. The play of an outer card releases the next in the column, i.e. a card is available if it has one narrower edge free. When you fill any space, you must fill all spaces that exist at that time; you may not pause during the deal to play upon foundations. All spaces must be filled eventually before a new row of ten is dealt, and they must be filled in strict order by rows, left to right, top to bottom. You have the option of building up or down as many, or as few, cards as you please to the foundations, before filling spaces.

If there is no space in the tableau, the turn of a card from the stock commits you to deal a new row of ten. In other words, you may not peek at the next card in order to decide whether to make a space.

Reversal When two foundations of the same suit meet, the top cards being in sequence, any or all cards may be reversed from one pile upon the other, except the ace or king at bottom.

BABETTE
Time required: 15 minutes
Chance of winning: 1 in 3 games

Layout Deal a row of eight cards to start the tableau. Continue dealing the tableau by rows of eight cards, keeping the columns aligned.

Foundations As they become available, move one ace and one king of each suit into a row above the tableau. Build the aces up in suit to kings and the kings down in suit to aces.

Play After dealing a tableau row, pause and play up what you can to the foundations. A tableau card is available if its lower edge is open, i.e. if it is at the bottom of a column or just above a gap in the column. Do not fill spaces at any time.

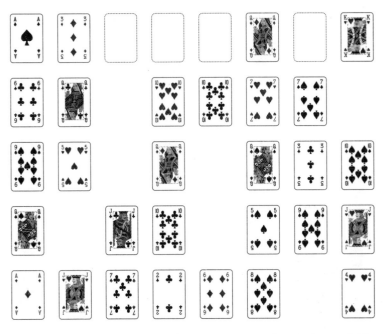

Babette at an advanced stage The ♥A, ♣A, ♠K and ♣K, when available, will be moved into the foundation (top) row. The ♥5, ♣10, ♠9 and all cards in the bottom row are available; there is no play for them, so another row of eight cards will be dealt below the bottom row.

Redeal One redeal is allowed. To form the new stock, slide the columns into piles without disturbing the order, and pick up the piles by putting each on its right-hand neighbour so that the one at the right becomes the top of the stock.

Tips To save room, overlap the cards in column, but keep track of the gaps. Look in each column for cards of the same suit and look for duplicate cards in different columns. Avoid playing a card from above a gap to a foundation until its duplicate has appeared.

FOUR INTRUDERS
Time required: 15 minutes
Chance of winning: 3 out of 4 games

Foundations Remove the eight aces from the pack and put them in a row. Build them up in suit to kings.

Layout Deal four cards in column at the left, forming the tableau. Below the foundations deal a row of eight cards, starting the reserve.

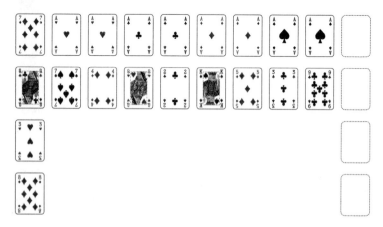

Four Intruders layout The column at the left is the tableau; the broken lines indicate the column in which the four 'intruders' will be dealt.

Play After making all possible plays with the first eight cards of the reserve, deal the rest of the stock, except the last four cards, in rows of eight to the reserve (not overlapping), pausing after each deal to play what you can.

Available reserve cards may be played on foundations or built on the tableau. A reserve card is available if its lower edge is free, i.e. if it is at the bottom of a column or just above a gap in the column. Never fill spaces in the reserve.

On the tableau, build down in suit. Move a whole tableau pile as a unit, for building on another pile. Top cards of tableau piles are available for building on foundations. Fill tableau spaces only from the reserve; such spaces must be filled before a new row is dealt to the reserve.

Intruders The last four cards of the pack are 'intruders'. Deal them in the column at the right. They are available for play on the foundations or tableau. Fill spaces in this column from the reserve. Once the intruders have been dealt, reserve cards may not be played to the tableau, but only to the intruder column or to foundations.

TRIUMPH
Time required: 15 minutes
Chance of winning: 1 in 2 games

Foundations Remove the eight aces from the pack and put them in a row. Build them up in suit to kings.

Layout Deal four cards in column at the left, forming the tableau. Below the foundations deal a row of eight cards, starting the reserve. (The layout is the same as that depicted for Four Intruders (page 152), except for the column at the right.)

Early play After making what plays you can with the first eight cards of the reserve, deal the rest of the stock to the reserve in rows of eight (not overlapping), pausing after each deal to make what plays you can. The bottom card of each reserve column is available for play on foundations. Spaces in the reserve must be filled from the stock, but you may defer filling a space to make other plays. All spaces must be filled before the next row of eight is dealt.

Tableau cards are available for play on foundations and may be built on each other down in suit. Move a whole tableau pile as a unit. A space in the tableau must be filled at once from the stock. (Note that reserve cards may not be moved into the tableau.)

Final play After the whole pack is dealt out, you may draw any four cards out of the reserve. The card above each gap thus created becomes available. Drawn cards may be built on the tableau as well as on foundations. A place must be found for each of the four cards so drawn, before another draw is made.

Two such draws, of four cards at a time, are allowed.

MISS MILLIGAN
Time required: 20 minutes
Chance of winning: 1 in 20 games

Layout Deal the whole pack in rows of eight cards, overlapping the rows to form piles of cards spread downwards, and pausing after each deal to play what you can.

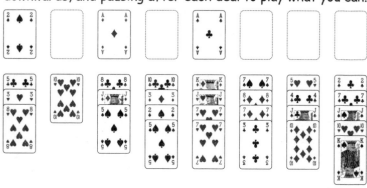

Miss Milligan after several plays The ♠2 has been built on the ♠A in the foundation row.

Foundations Move the eight aces, as they become available, to a foundation row. Build them up in suit to kings.

Play The top cards of the tableau piles are available for play on foundations and on each other. On the tableau, build down in alternate colours. All cards at the top of the pile, in correct suit and sequence, may be lifted as a unit to be built elsewhere.

A space made by clearing away an entire pile may be filled only by an available king.

Weaving After the whole pack is dealt, you may lift up any available card or build from the tableau and set it aside as a reserve, of which all cards are available. After these cards are built back into the layout, on foundations or tableau, you may similarly set aside another available card or batch of available cards. You may continue this 'weaving' process until the game is won, or until you find no place for a card set aside.

BLOCKADE
Time required: 15 minutes
Chance of winning: 3 out of 4 games

Layout Deal 12 piles, one row at a time, pausing after each deal of 12 cards to play what you can.

Blockade layout The ♠A and broken lines indicate the foundation row. The ♠2 may be built on ♠A, ♥3 on ♥4 and ♥2 on ♥3, ♠10 on ♠J.

Foundations Move the eight aces, as they become available, to a row above the tableau. Build them up in suit to kings.

Play The top card of each tableau pile is available for play on foundations, or on the top card of another tableau pile, building down in suit. All cards in correct suit and sequence, at the top of a pile, may be lifted as a unit to be built elsewhere.

A space in the tableau may be filled by any available card or build from the tableau or from the stock. All spaces must be filled before a new row of 12 cards is dealt on the tableau.

STAG PARTY
Time required: 15 minutes
Chance of winning: 2 out of 3 games

Layout Deal a row of eight cards to start the tableau. Continue dealing the tableau by rows of eight cards, keeping the columns aligned.

Foundations As they become available, move all fives and sixes to foundation columns on each side of the tableau. Build the sixes up in suit to jacks and the fives down in suit to aces, then kings.

Play After dealing a tableau row, pause and play up what you can to the foundations. A tableau card is available if its lower

155

edge is not covered, i.e. if it is at the bottom of a column or just above a gap in the column. Do not fill spaces at any time.

Discard all queens as soon as they are dealt, leaving gaps in their places.

Tips To save room, overlap the cards in the column, but keep track of the gaps.

GARGANTUA
(Double Klondike)
Time required: 20 minutes
Chance of winning: 1 in 2 games

Layout Deal 45 cards in a tableau of nine piles, increasing from one card to nine per pile. Only the top card of each pile should be face up, the remaining cards being dealt face down. The usual method of dealing is by rows.

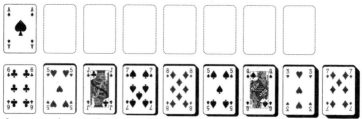

Gargantua layout The ♣A and broken lines indicate the foundation row.

Foundations Move the aces, as they become available, to a row above the tableau. Build them up in suit to kings.

Tableau On the tableau, build down in alternate colours. The top card or all face-up cards may be removed from a pile as a unit to be built elsewhere. On baring a face-down card, turn it up; it then becomes available.

A space made by clearing away an entire pile may be filled only by an available king (with or without a build on it).

Play Turn up cards from the stock one at a time, putting unplayable cards in a single wastepile, the top card of which is available.

Redeal One redeal is allowed.

ST HELENA
(Napoleon's Favourite, Washington's Favourite)
Time required: 20 minutes
Chance of winning: 9 out of 10 games

Foundations Remove from the pack one ace and one king of each suit and put them in two rows. Build the aces up in suit to kings and the kings down in suit to aces.

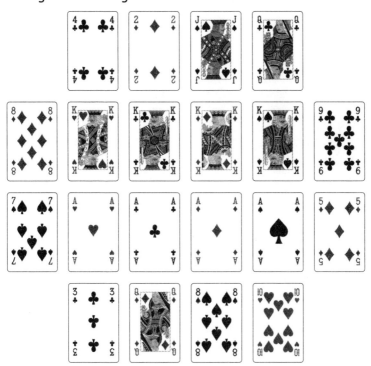

St Helena layout The kings and aces are foundations, set out in advance. The ♣Q may be built on the ♣K, but not ♦2 on ♦A or ♦Q on ♦K. However, the ♦Q may be built on ♠J and then on ♦K; and ♦2 on ♣3 and then on ♦A. The ♥10 may be built on ♠J, then ♣9, ♦8 or ♠8, ♠7, then the other eight.

Tableau Deal the rest of the pack into 12 piles around the foundations – a row of four above and below, and a column of two at each side. Deal to the piles one card at a time in clockwise rotation, beginning at the left end of the top row.

157

Play Top cards of the tableau piles are available for building on foundations, with this restriction in the original deal: from the top row, cards may be moved only to king-foundations; from the bottom row, to ace-foundations only; from the side columns, to any foundations.

Tableau cards may also be built on each other, up or down regardless of suit. You may reverse direction on the same pile. But sequence of rank is not continuous: only a queen may be built on a king, only a two on an ace. One card at a time may be lifted from the top of a pile for transfer elsewhere.

Redeals Two redeals are allowed. To form the new stock, pick up the 12 tableau piles in reverse order, the left-hand pile of the top row on its right-hand neighbour, and so on in clockwise rotation, so that the last-dealt will be at the top when the stock is turned face down.

After each redeal, the top card of any pile may be played off to any foundation.

LOUIS
(St Louis, Newport)
Time required: 20 minutes
Chance of winning: 9 out of 10 games

Follow all the rules of St Helena except as modified: after dealing the first 12 cards to the tableau, you may pause and play up what you can to the foundations, filling spaces at once from the stock; but thereafter you must deal out the whole stock before resuming play. In all deals, all top cards of tableau piles are available for play anywhere. Building on the tableau may be up or down, but must be in suit.

NAPOLEON'S SQUARE

Time required: 8 minutes
Chance of winning: 9 out of 10 games

Layout Deal a tableau of 48 cards, in 12 piles of four cards each, around three sides of a square. Deal the cards either one or four at a time to each pile in rotation.

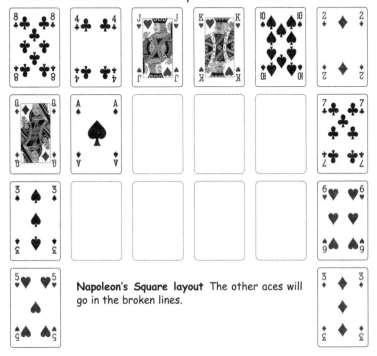

Napoleon's Square layout The other aces will go in the broken lines.

Foundations Move the eight aces, as they become available, to the centre area. Build them up in suit to kings.

Play On the tableau, build down in suit. All cards at the top of a pile that are in correct sequence may be lifted as a unit to be built elsewhere. A space made by clearing away an entire pile may be filled by any available card or build, from tableau, wastepile or stock.

Turn up cards from the stock one at a time, putting unplayable cards in a single wastepile, the top card of which is always available. There is no redeal.

Tableau piles may be spread for examination.

DEUCES

Time required: 10 minutes
Chance of winning: 1 in 2 games

Foundations Remove the eight twos and put them in two rows. Build them up in suit to aces, which rank highest.

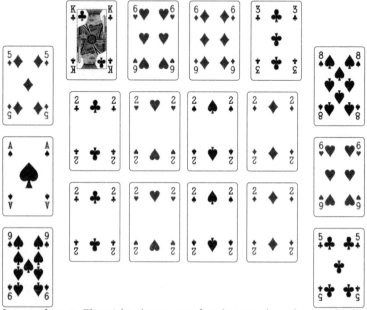

Deuces layout The eight deuces are foundations, the other cards the tableau. The ♣3 may be built on ♣2, ♠8 on ♠9, ♦5 on ♦6; the ♠K, if available, could be built on the ♠A.

Tableau Deal ten cards around three sides of the foundations – four above, and three on each side.

On the tableau, build down in suit. The top card of a pile is available; or any or all cards in proper sequence at the top may be moved as a unit to be built on the top card of another pile. Fill spaces at once from wastepile or stock (never from tableau).

Play Turn up cards from the stock one at a time, playing them on foundations or tableau. Put unplayable cards in a single wastepile, the top card of which is available for play to foundations or tableau.

SQUARE
(Pluto)
Time required: 10 minutes
Chance of winning: 1 in 2 games

Follow all the rules for Deuces, except: do not remove the twos from the pack at the outset; move them into position as they become available. Deal 12 cards for the tableau, putting four cards in each column.

COURTYARD
Time required: 10 minutes
Chance of winning: 1 in 2 games

This is the same game as Square, using aces for foundations instead of twos.

BRITISH SQUARE
Time required: 8 minutes
Chance of winning: 5 out of 6 games

Layout Deal a tableau of 16 cards, in four rows of four each.

Foundations As they become available, move one ace of each suit to a row above the tableau. Build them up in suit to kings, then add the duplicate kings on them and build down in suit to aces.

Play On the top cards of tableau piles, build in suit up or down as you please. Once a build is made, it fixes the direction of building for that pile; the direction may not be reversed by later cards. One card at a time may be moved from the top of a tableau pile; thus one pile may be reversed on another. A build on the tableau ends with an ace or king.

A space in the tableau may be filled only from wastepile or stock. You may look at the next card from the stock, to decide whether to move it or the top of the wastepile into a space.

Turn up cards from the stock one at a time, putting unplayable cards in a single wastepile, the top card of which is always available. There is no redeal.

Tips More convenient for examination of the tableau piles is to deal them in two rows of eight cards each, and spread the piles downwards as you build them.

Avoid building duplicates in the same direction, unless there is good prospect of later reversing one build. Don't forget that the foundation in each suit goes up first, down later. This means that from the tableau you will have to play off first the down-builds, and then later the up-builds. Don't move the whole of a down-build to the foundation until you have checked that all the remaining cards of the same suit in the tableau lie in up-builds.

CRESCENT
Time required: 20 minutes
Chance of winning: 9 out of 10 games

Foundations Remove from the pack one ace and one king of each suit and put these foundations in one or two rows.

Build the aces up in suit to kings and the kings down in suit to aces.

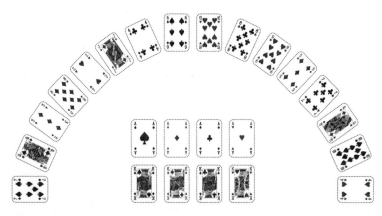

Crescent layout The aces and kings are foundations, set out in advance. The tableau piles, shown here in traditional crescent form, may more conveniently be set out in rows.

Tableau Deal the rest of the pack into 16 piles of six cards each, arranged in a semicircle around the foundations. (This traditional arrangement gives the game its name. The normal-size folding card table is too small for it. It is more convenient to deal two straight rows of eight piles each.)

The top card of each pile should be dealt face up, the remaining cards face down.

Play Top cards of the tableau piles are available for play on foundations and also for building on each other. On the tableau, build in suit, up or down as you please. You may reverse direction on the same pile. Sequence of rank is continuous, ace being below the two and above the king. Only one card at a time may be lifted from a pile to be played elsewhere.

On baring a face-down card, turn it up; it then becomes available. Never fill spaces made by clearing away entire piles.

Reversal When two foundations of the same suit meet, the top cards being in sequence, any or all cards of one pile may be reversed upon the other, except the ace or king at the bottom.

Shifts When play comes to a standstill, make a *shift:* move the bottom card of every tableau pile to the top. Three such shifts are allowed. (Note that the shift must be made in every pile, not merely in those piles containing face-down cards. It thus disarranges the builds on piles where the cards are all face up.)

Tips Only extraordinary bad luck can defeat you, but be careful in building to avoid defeating yourself. Watch the direction of all builds, in order to make all necessary reversals before it is too late. For example, if you have built both ♣5s on both ♣6s, one of these pairs must be reversed sooner or later to be playable on a foundation. Yet, you cannot avoid making parallel builds, because the paramount consideration is to get all buried cards into play. The safest general principles are: (1) avoid changing direction of build on a pile unless you are certain that you can split the pile later into two one-way builds; (2) play to a foundation only when compelled in order to get at buried cards, or you can see that the card played is no longer needed in the tableau; (3) hold every pair of foundations at the meeting point until you are sure that all remaining cards of the suit lie in sequences of the right direction to be playable. The point of the last instruction is that the reversal privilege is invaluable to dissolve a final 'snarl-up' in the builds.

SULTAN
(Sultan of Turkey, Emperor of Germany)
Time required: 10 minutes
Chance of winning: 2 out of 3 games

Foundations Remove the eight kings and one ♥A from the pack. Put them in three rows of three, with a ♥K in the centre and the ♥A below it. Do not build on the central ♥K. On all the other kings, build up in suit to queens, the ace ranking between king and two. Likewise build the ♥A up in suit to the ♥Q.

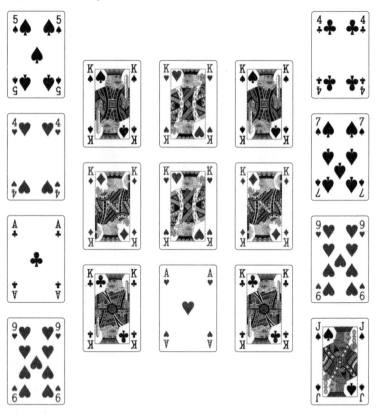

Sultan layout The kings and ♥A are foundations; there is no building on the ♥K in the centre.

Reserve Deal a column of four cards on each side of the foundations, forming the 'divan'. All cards of the divan are available for play on the foundations. A space must be filled at once from the wastepile, or, if there is no wastepile, from the stock.

Play Turn up cards from the stock one at a time, putting unplayable cards in a single wastepile. The top of this pile is always available.

Redeals Two redeals are allowed.

EIGHTEENS
(Ferris Wheel, The Wheel)
Time required: 8 minutes
Chance of winning: 1 in 30 games

Deal three rows of four cards each. From this tableau discard aces singly; discard other cards in groups of four, comprising one face card (king, queen or jack) together with three lower cards that total 18. But no group may contain two cards of the same rank (e.g. as three sixes, or two sevens and a four). Fill spaces in the tableau at once from the stock. The game is won if you succeed in discarding the whole pack.

PATRIARCHS
Time required: 8 minutes
Chance of winning: 1 in 20 games

Foundations Remove one ace and one king of each suit from the pack. Put the aces in a column at the left, the kings in a column at the right. Build the aces up in suit and the kings down in suit. When the top cards of two foundation piles of the same suit are in sequence, any or all the cards of one pile may be reversed upon the other, except for the ace or king at the bottom.

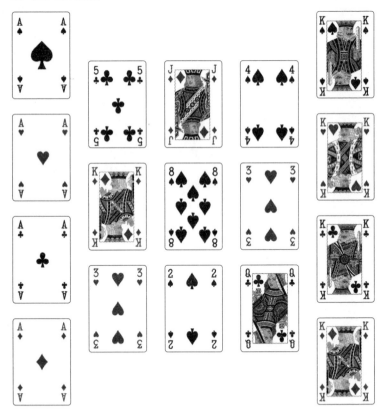

Patriarchs layout The columns of aces and kings are foundations, set out in advance; the cards in the centre are the reserve. The ♣Q may be built on the ♣K, and the ♠2 on the ♠A.

Reserve Between the foundation columns, deal three rows of three cards each, forming the reserve. All cards of the reserve are available for play on foundations. Spaces must be filled at once from the wastepile, or, if there is none, from the stock.

Play Turn up cards from the stock one at a time, putting unplayable cards in a single wastepile. The top card of the wastepile is always available.

Redeal One redeal is allowed.

ROYAL RENDEZVOUS
Time required: 20 minutes
Chance of winning: 2 out of 3 games

Layout Remove from the pack four twos of different suits, also the eight aces. Put four aces of different suits in a row (I) and their duplicates in a row below (II). Add the twos in row II, two at each end. Below these two rows of foundations, deal 16 cards in a reserve, two rows of eight each.

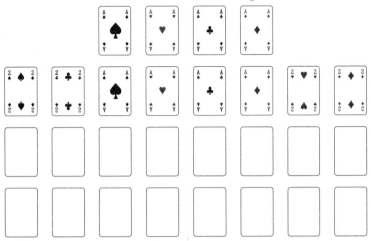

Royal Rendezvous layout The aces and twos are foundations, set out in advance; the outlines represent face-up cards in the reserve.

Foundations Build the aces of row I up in suit to queens. Build the aces of row II up in suit by twos thus: A, 3, 5, 6, 9, J, K. Build the twos up in suit by twos, as follows: 2, 4, 6, 8, 10, Q.

Play All cards of the reserve are available for play on foundations. Spaces must be filled at once from the wastepile, or, if there is none, from the stock.

Turn up cards from the stock one at a time, putting unplayable cards in a single wastepile, the top card of which is always available. There is no redeal.

Four of the kings are not built on foundations. Put them in row I to complete the final picture, with the proviso that a king may be so placed only after its duplicate has been built in row II.

BIG BEN
(Clock)
Time required: 20 minutes
Chance of winning: 1 in 2 games

Layout Remove from the pack the following 12 cards: ♣2, ♥3, ♠4, ♦5, ♣6, ♥7, ♠8, ♦9, ♣10, ♥J, ♠Q and ♦K. Arrange them in a circle corresponding to the hours on a clock, with the ♣2 at 'nine o'clock' and the rest in sequence clockwise.

Around the rim of the clock deal 12 fans of three cards each. These cards form the tableau.

Big Ben layout The centre circle of cards constitutes the foundations; the outside cards the tableau. The ♥Q may be built on the ♥J; the ♣J on the ♣10, and the ♥8 uncovered by the ♣J goes on the ♥7. The exposed ♦6, 7 and 8 may be built on the ♦5 in the centre, and the ♠9 on the ♠8. Additional plays are then possible on both the foundations and the tableau.

169

Foundations The 12 cards in the circle are foundations. Build each up in suit until the top card of the pile shows the number corresponding to its position on the dial. For example, build the ♣2 up to the ♣9. Thus, seven more cards are wanted on the ♣2, ♥3, ♠4 and ♦5, while eight more are wanted on each of the other foundations.

Tableau Top cards of tableau fans (one card at a time) may be lifted for building on foundations or on each other. On the tableau, build down in suit, rank being continuous (ace below the two and above the king).

Each fan must be maintained at a minimum of three cards. The 'spaces' in a fan of less than three cards must be filled from the stock (never from the wastepile or tableau). They need not be filled immediately; you may continue to build on foundations and tableau, with spaces in abeyance. But if you fill any space, you must fill all spaces that exist at that time. Furthermore, you must fill them in strict rotation. Beginning at '12 o'clock', restore the first short pile to three cards, then serve the next in rotation clockwise, and so on.

Play Turn up cards from the stock one at a time, putting unplayable cards in a single wastepile. The top of the wastepile is always available for play on foundations, or for building (not filling a space) on the tableau.

Tips Examine the fans for reversed sequences – a card covering a lower card of the same suit, whether or not other cards intervene. Plan the play to break up such reversals before they become fatal blocks. Do not be hasty in playing to the foundations.

CONTRADANCE
(Cotillion)
Time required: 5 minutes
Chance of winning: 1 in 20 games

Foundations Remove the fives and sixes from the pack and put them in two rows. Build the sixes up in suit to queens, and the fives down in suit to aces, then kings.

Play Turn up cards from the stock one at a time, putting unplayable cards in a single wastepile. The top card of the wastepile is always available.

Redeal One redeal is allowed.

EVICTING
Time required: 3 minutes
Chance of winning: 1 in 20 games

Deal cards in one row from left to right. Whenever two cards, separated by two others, are alike in suit or rank, discard the intervening cards. Keep the gaps closed up by moving the cards leftwards without changing their order. You win the game if you have reduced the row to two cards after the last card has been dealt.

RUSSIAN BANK
(Crapette)

Russian Bank is a game for two players, resembling double solitaire in that the object of play is to build on foundations. But it differs from other double solitaires in that the contestants play alternately, instead of simultaneously. Furthermore, the play is governed by strict rules of procedure, violation of which ends the player's turn.

Packs Each player is provided with a regulation pack of 52 cards, which rank as in other solitaires (ace low).

Preliminaries One pack is spread face down, and each player draws a card. The lower card gives the right to play first. Each player then shuffles the pack to be used by their opponent.

Layout Each player deals a pile of 12 cards face down at his right, forming his reserve. He then deals a column of four cards face up, above the reserve. The two columns dealt in this way form the tableau and can be played by both players.

Foundations Every ace, as it becomes available, must be moved to the *centre*. Aces are built up in suit to kings.

Tableau building Tableau cards may be built down in alternate colours. Available for this purpose are other tableau cards (only the top card of a pile), the top of the reserve, and a card turned up from the stock. Only one card at a time may be lifted from a tableau pile for building elsewhere. A space may be filled from the tableau or from the reserve, or when the reserve is exhausted, it may be filled from the stock.

Commencing play At his first turn, the player must begin by making all possible plays from tableau to centre (foundations). Then he must turn the top card of his reserve face up. At all later turns, the player is entitled to turn up the top of his reserve (if it chances to be face down), before making any play.

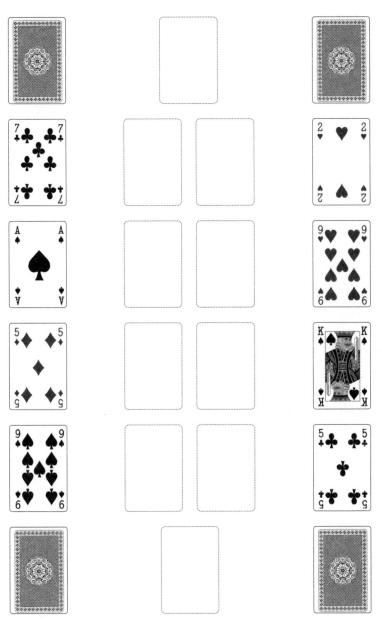

Russian Bank layout At the player's right is his reserve; at left, his stock. Between the two he will place his wastepile. The columns on each side are the tableau. Broken lines in the centre show where the aces will go.

The reserve The top card of the reserve must be played to the centre ahead of any playable card in the tableau. But in building and filling spaces on the tableau, other tableau cards or the reserve card may be used in any order. Of course, spaces are held open to make it easier to release wanted cards, but eventually the player gets rid of as many reserve cards as he can into the tableau.

The stock When no play to the centre is possible, and his reserve card cannot be put into the tableau, the player may turn up the top card of his stock. This proviso means that all tableau spaces must be filled prior to the turn from stock, but it does not mean that the player is bound to make all possible tableau builds and fill all possible spaces.

The stock card is available for play on foundations or tableau. If it is so played, the next stock card may be turned up under the same rule – that no play can be made to the centre and the reserve card is immovable. The player's turn continues so long as he can play the cards he turns from the stock. When he reaches an unplayable card, it must be laid face up on his *wastepile,* and his turn ends. The act of laying a card on his wastepile ends his turn, even though he instantly realises that the card could have been played.

Wastepile Cards on the wastepile may *never* be removed for any purpose. But after his stock is exhausted, the player turns over his wastepile to form a new stock.

Loading A player may *load* his opponent's reserve card and also his wastepile, by building on them in suit, up or down. Available for this purpose are cards from the tableau, his own reserve and stock. If the opponent has failed to turn up the top card of his reserve when his turn ends, he may be asked to turn it up at any time.

Procedure To recapitulate the rules of procedure:
(1) A play to the centre takes precedence over all else, except the act (on a later turn) of turning up the top card of the reserve.
(2) In play to the centre, the reserve takes precedence over tableau and stock.

(3) The stock card may not be turned up so long as the reserve card is playable. It is playable if a space in fact exists in the tableau, but is not deemed playable because a space could be made by manipulation.

(4) Except as above, there is no order of precedence among plays from reserve to tableau, builds and space-making in the tableau, loading the opponent.

(5) A stock card is playable only if it can be laid on a tableau or centre pile, or loaded on the opponent's reserve or wastepile. It is not playable if further manipulation of the tableau could make place for it on tableau or centre. An unplayable stock card must be laid on the wastepile; it is no longer available, and the player's turn ends.

Stops If a player makes any error of procedure under the foregoing rules, his opponent may cry 'Stop!'. Play must cease on any such call. If the error can then be proved, the player's turn ends.

Among some players, a false call of 'Stop!' is penalised: one card face down is transferred from the player's reserve to the offender's reserve.

There are different rules about when an error can be said to have been made and when it cannot be said. The strictest rule is that it is an error to touch any card, except in saying 'I arrange', when another card should have been played ahead of it. It is generally agreed that a player may not be stopped if he has been able to finish another play after the one in which he committed the error.

Scoring The first player to get rid of his entire reserve and stock into the tableau and foundations wins the game. He scores 30 for winning, plus one point for each card left in the opponent's stock and wastepile, and two points for each card left in his reserve; including all cards that have been loaded on these piles.

SOLITAIRES PLAYED WITH STRIPPED PACKS

AMAZONS
Time required: 5 minutes
Chance of winning: 1 in 10 games

Pack Discard from the pack all kings, twos, threes, fours, fives and sixes. The remaining cards rank: Q (high), J, 10, 9, 8, 7, A (low).

Layout Deal a row of four cards to start the reserve.

Foundations Move the four aces, as they become available, to a row above the reserve. Lay them strictly left to right in the order in which they become available. Build them up in suit to queens.

Play The top of each reserve pile is available for play only on the foundation immediately above it, except that a queen may be played from any pile. Do not fill spaces except by the ensuing deal. Continue to deal the entire stock upon the reserve, four cards at a time, one on each pile. Pause after each deal to play up what you can.

Redeals Redeal without limit until the game is won or ends in a block. To form the new stock, gather the reserve piles, each upon its left-hand neighbour; turn over and deal without shuffling.

EVEN UP
Time required: 2 minutes
Chance of winning: 1 in 3 games

Discard from the pack all face cards – kings, queens and jacks.

Deal cards one at a time in a single overlapping row. Remove and discard any two adjacent cards whose numerical total is an even number. After each discard, close the gap in the row and look to see if there is an added play at the junction. You win the game if you succeed in discarding the entire pack.

LITTLE LOTS
Time required: 1 minute
Chance of winning: 1 in 6 games

Pack Discard from the pack all twos, threes, fours, fives and sixes.

Layout Deal the whole pack in eight piles of four cards each, face down.

Play Turn the top card of each pile. Discard these cards in pairs of the same rank. Turn up the next card of each pile from which a card is discarded, and continue pairing. When two cards have been removed from any pile, both of the last two may be turned up, and if they are a pair they may be discarded. You win the game if you succeed in discarding the entire pack.

KNOCKOUT
(Hope Deferred)
Time required: 3 minutes
Chance of winning: 1 in 3 games

Discard from the pack all twos, threes, fours, fives and sixes.

Deal a row of three cards. If any are clubs, discard them and fill the spaces from the stock. Continue dealing three cards at a time, one on each pile. After each deal, discard any clubs that show. Fill a space (removal of an entire pile) at once with one card from the stock. Cease play after you have made five complete deals of three (15 cards plus any dealt to fill spaces).

Gather all the cards exclusive of discarded clubs, shuffle them and commence dealing again in the same way. Two such redeals are allowed.

To win the game you must get all eight clubs into the discard pile.

XERXES
Time required: 5 minutes
Chance of winning: 1 in 3 games

Pack Shuffle two packs after discarding all cards from twos to eights inclusive. (That is, use a Pinochle pack of 48 cards, two cards of each rank from nine to ace in each suit.)

Layout Remove any nine and put it at the left. Below it deal cards in a pile, spread downwards, until you turn up another nine. Put this to the right of the first nine and start a new pile below it. Continue dealing the entire pack in the same way, putting all nines in a row and starting a new pile below each.

Play The nines are foundations. Build them up, regardless of suits, to aces. The top card of every tableau pile is available. There is no building on the tableau, only on the foundations. A space made by removing an entire pile may be filled by the top card of any other pile.

ZINGARA
Time required: 5 minutes
Chance of winning: 1 in 3 games

Pack Shuffle two packs after discarding all twos, threes, fours, fives and sixes.

Layout Remove any seven and put it at the left. Below it start dealing cards in a pile, spread downward. When you turn another seven, put it to the right of the first and start dealing a new pile below it. Deal out the whole pack in the same way, putting all sevens in a row and starting a new pile beneath each.

Play The sevens are foundations. Build them up, regardless of suit, to aces.

While dealing the layout, you may put any eight or nine turned from the stock on a foundation. But you may play up no higher card until the deal is complete and until that time you may not move any card already dealt to the layout.

The deal finished, the top card of every pile is available for play on foundations.

A space made by removing an entire pile may be filled by the top card from any other pile.

BOOMERANG
Time required: 5 minutes
Chance of winning: 1 in 2 games

Pack Shuffle two packs together after removing all twos, threes, fours, fives and sixes.

Layout Deal a tableau of 12 cards, in three rows of four cards each.

Foundations As they become available, move one seven of each suit into a row above the tableau. Build these foundations in suit as follows: 7, 8, 9, 10, J, Q, K, A, K, Q, J, 10, 9, 8, 7, A.

Play A single tableau card (not one of a pile) may be built upon another card or pile, up or down in suit. The direction of the first build must be followed in all subsequent builds on the same pile. Owing to the sequence on the foundations, in the tableau an ace may be built only on a king, but either a king or a seven may be built on an ace.

The top cards of all tableau piles are available for play on foundations.

Fill each space in the tableau from the stock, never from another tableau pile. Turn cards up from the stock one at a time (to see the card before deciding how to make a space). Continue play so long as each successive card can be added to the foundations or the tableau, by building or by filling a space. If you turn a card, for which you are unable to make a place, the game is lost.

Tips The ideal build starts with a king on an ace. Having started a build, you may as well carry it on as far as you can, since a space can be made there only by playing off the whole pile on a foundation. But there is one exception to this rule, noted below.

Boomerang layout The lower three rows are the tableau. The foundations, one seven of each suit, are placed above, in the spaces indicated by the broken lines, as they become available. The outlines represent face-up cards.

Of course, it is imperative to avoid building duplicate cards in the same direction. For example, if you have put a jack on a queen, you will create an impasse if you build the duplicate jack on the duplicate queen. Now consider another situation: you have made builds of Q–J and J–10 of the same suit. You naturally try to avoid having a common card in two builds in the same direction. But perhaps you could not help yourself: you have to lay the second jack on the queen to continue play. To avoid a block you must later play off the ten on a foundation, followed by the jack that lies on the queen. If you play the jack that was under the ten, you leave the other build in the wrong direction. (Of course, it would be fatal to put the duplicate ten on the open jack, for then you would have two J–10 builds.)

In the early play, build down on the tableau, since such builds will be wanted on foundations before the up-builds. But as soon as the tableau contains the duplicate of a card already on the foundations, use it for an up-build. For example, having moved a ♣7 to the foundation row, when the other ♣7 appears, build it as soon as possible on an ♣A, and then continue with ♣8, ♣9, etc. The ideal builds start from aces as end cards; the most dangerous are those based on middle cards, especially tens and jacks, since they jeopardise potential spaces.

SUDDEN DEATH

This is the same game as Boomerang, using a Pinochle pack of 48 cards (i.e. two regular packs from which are discarded all cards from twos to eights inclusive, and so consisting of two cards of each rank from nine to ace in each suit). The nines are foundations and the sequence built on them is: 9, 10, J, Q, K, A, K, Q, J, 10, 9. A. Make the tableau only ten piles, in two rows of five each.

OLGA
Time required: 30 minutes
Chance of winning: 3 out of 4 games

Pack From each of four packs discard all twos, threes, fours, fives and sixes.

Layout Deal a tableau of 49 cards in seven rows of seven cards each. Lay all the cards in the second, fourth and sixth rows face down; all others face up.

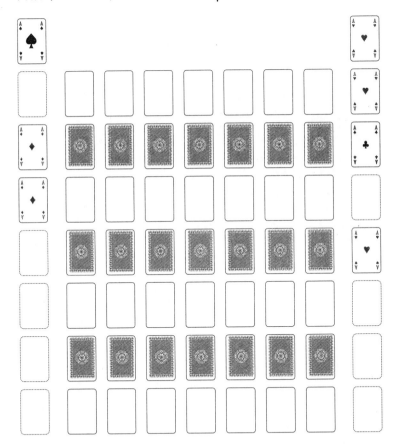

Olga layout The second, fourth and sixth rows of the tableau are dealt face down. Foundation aces are placed at the side, as they become available during the deal and play. The outlines represent face-up cards; the broken lines, the spaces to be occupied by the other aces.

Foundations Move the 16 aces, as they become available, to two columns on each side of the tableau. Build them up in suit to kings. (Aces are low; next-higher are sevens.)

If in dealing the layout you turn up an ace, or a card playable on a foundation, you may put it there instead of in the tableau. But a card once laid in the tableau may not be moved until the deal is complete. Do not leave any spaces in the tableau because of cards played up to foundations; give the tableau its full quota of 49 cards.

Play All face-up cards in the tableau are available to be built on each other. On the tableau, build down in alternate colours. All cards or any number of cards from the top of a pile may be moved as a unit to be built elsewhere.

Only the bottom available card of each column may be played on foundations. When a face-down card is at the bottom of a column, turn it up; it then becomes available. (Note that the removal of a face-down card in the interior of a column does not release the card above the gap.)

A space made by clearing away an entire column may be filled by any available king from either the tableau or wastepile.

Turn cards up from the stock one at a time, putting unplayable cards in a single wastepile. The top of this pile is always available for play on foundations or tableau.

Tips Commence by building in the tableau to release all possible cards and also to make a space. Any king blocks access to the cards above it in column; winning the game depends primarily on making enough spaces to get all such kings out of the way.

As a rule, build on foundations not when you can but when you must, e.g. when you must get a blocking king out of the way by foundation-play. Save low cards from being buried in the wastepile; to do so, keep middling-high cards in the tableau until they are no longer needed. Don't overlook that cards higher in a column can often be made playable on foundations by temporary transfer to the bottom row.

EMPRESS OF INDIA
Time required: 30 minutes
Chance of winning: 9 out of 10 games

Pack Shuffle together four complete packs, making 208 cards in all.

Layout Remove from the pack the eight black queens, the eight red jacks, the eight red kings and the eight black aces. Put the queens in a pile in the centre, with the ♣Q on top; put the jacks in a circle around this pile. (This part of the layout is purely ornamental. The ♣Q represents the Empress of India, and the red jacks, her guards. You can save space by discarding these cards entirely.) Put the black aces and red kings in two concentric circles around the jacks.

Deal a tableau of 48 cards, in four rows of 12 cards each. All cards of the upper two rows, the 'army', must be red, and all of the lower two rows, the 'navy', black. In dealing, put each card in the section of its own colour, and if any excess of either colour is turned up, put these cards in the wastepile.

Foundations Build the black aces up in suit to kings and the red kings down in suit to aces. Owing to the discard of the black queens and red jacks, the black foundations will skip from jack to kings and the red will skip from queens to tens.

Corresponding cards

Black:	A	2	3	4	5	6	7	8	9	10	J	K
Red:	K	Q	10	9	8	7	6	5	4	3	2	A

Play Cards may be moved to the foundations only from the tableau, and then only in couples of corresponding cards, one red and one black. The couples are shown by the columns of the foregoing table – a black two and a red queen, etc. Fill a space in the tableau at once from the top of the wastepile of same colour (see diagram on next page).

Spaces may be made in the tableau by building any card, red or black, on its corresponding card of opposite colour (as shown in the table). Later the build may be picked up and distributed upon two foundations.

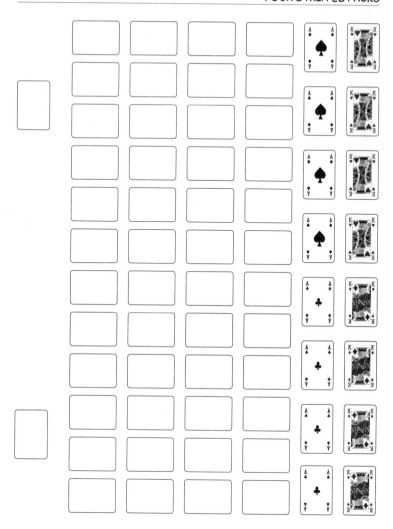

Empress of India layout This layout has been consolidated to take less room than the traditional layout described in the text. The ornamental part is omitted. Foundation kings and aces are turned sideways. The upper two rows of the tableau, all red cards are the 'army'; the lower two rows, all black, are the 'navy'. At the bottom is one wastepile of each colour. The outlines represent face-up cards.

Turn up cards from the stock one at a time, putting them in two wastepiles, one red and one black. These cards may be brought into play only through spaces in the 'army' and 'navy'.

INDEX